# Modern Business

## Its Friends & Foes

# Modern Business

## Its Friends & Foes

J.R. Zyla

Viva Books

New Delhi | Mumbai | Chennai | Kolkata | Bengaluru | Hyderabad | Kochi | Guwahati

**First Indian Edition 2014**

**VIVA BOOKS PRIVATE LIMITED**

- 4737/23 Ansari Road, Daryaganj, New Delhi 110 002
  E-mail: vivadelhi@vivagroupindia.net, Tel. 42242200
- 76, Service Industries, Shirvane, Sector 1, Nerul, Navi Mumbai 400 706
  E-mail: vivamumbai@vivagroupindia.net, Tel. 27721273, 27721274
- Megh Towers, Old No. 307, New No. 165, Poonamallee High Road, Maduravoyal Chennai - 600 095 E-mail: vivachennai@vivagroupindia.net, Tel. 23780991, 23780992
- B-103, Jindal Towers, 21/1A/3 Darga Road, Kolkata 700 017
  E-mail: vivakolkata@vivagroupindia.net, Tel. 22836381, 22816713
- 7, Sovereign Park Apartments, 56-58, K. R. Road, Basavanagudi, Bengaluru 560 004
  E-mail: vivabangalore@vivagroupindia.net, Tel. 26607409, 26607410
- 101-102 Mughal Marc Apartments, 3-4-637 to 641, Narayanguda, Hyderabad 500 029
  E-mail: vivahyderabad@vivagroupindia.net, Tel. 27564481, 27564482
- Beevi Towers, First Floor, SRM Road, Kaloor, Kochi 682 018, Kerala
  E-mail: vivakochi@vivagroupindia.net, Tel: 0484-2403055, 2403056
- 232, GNB Road, Beside UCO Bank, Silpukhuri, Guwahati 781 003
  E-mail: vivaguwahati@vivagroupindia.net, Tel: 0361-2666386

*www.vivagroupindia.com*

*Published by arrangement with*
LID Publishing
6-8, Underwood Street
London N1 7JQ
UK



ISBN : 978-81-309-2679-7

Published by Vinod Vasishtha for Viva Books Private Limited, 4737/23, Ansari Road, Daryaganj, New Delhi - 110 002.

Printed and bound by Saku Printing House, New Delhi.

# Contents

# Welcome note

Let us be honest, at least to ourselves: does the modern corporate world, especially in times of crisis, resemble what we associate with heaven? Is working in business a heavenly experience or has it increasingly become the opposite? The answer is obvious – and with mounting business and performance pressures there seems no quick improvement in sight.

Given that we are *de facto* forced to work in this tough, demanding and often unforgiving system, it is only logical to ask the question: who had a vested interest in creating business this way, and why?

If, as we shall assume, the Devil really did have a hand in creating modern business life, then he did a most effective job. That is why we need to understand what he did, and how he did it, in order to improve our personal business life.

Despite its witty and provocative title this book is the result of many years of analytical work and detailed research; of speaking – often on a very personal basis – to thousands of senior business executives; and of personal observations across a large number of industries. It is written from the front line, drawing on the real experiences of real executives, and it is created for people in business who feel a need to review, reassess or possibly to reconstruct their own business life.

This book is also written because of a serious concern. Concern about the *real* state of our western industrialised business world.

That *real* state is not a happy one. Why? Because of socio-economic and personal-emotional factors. These determining factors are hard to calculate in economic and financial models, but they are easily felt and clearly recognizable by business executives, around the world, every day.

**Business people everywhere, not only in executive management, are often working at their physical and emotional limits; they feel exhausted, beleaguered by stress and frustration. Many executives on *all* corporate levels and many employees in companies do not see or feel the sense of it all anymore.**

This book will start by critically evaluating our current business philosophies and management values and how they relate, quite directly, to our concepts of God and the Devil, of good and evil.

The terms God and Devil are, of course, not used in a religious sense, rather as focused metaphors. But their influence as operating energies in business is considerably more powerful than we either think or realize – or are made to believe.

**We intuitively know that we live in decisive times that force each one of us in business or management to differentiate between good and bad – or more specifically, between what is good and bad *for us*.**

**The first part of the book therefore deals with *why* we should urgently do exactly that, i.e. analyse what helps us and what hurts us. The second part will suggest a number of actionable solutions.**

Your world starts and ends in one single place. That place is you, and your life. Take a good look at what you are doing with it. And if you don't like it, then go and change it!

If this is your goal, this book *will* help you to achieve it.

**JRZyla**
July 2010

# A provocative foreword

Let us imagine that there is a God. And then let us imagine that there is a Devil. And somewhere, probably right in the middle, lives an interesting, mixed life form, called a business executive.

For reasons we shall explore together in this book it seems that the Devil actually did use that tiny fraction of a moment in the creative process – just when God wasn't fully watching – in order to create a whole world, a world to *his* liking, the world of business.

As we go along, you will swiftly understand how it all works. You may be surprised, possibly even shocked.

You see, judging by the status of today's business world – or rather more precisely, the world of business created by us human beings – the Devil's level of efficiency was no less than superb.

Worse than that, the Devil as a creative energy set it all up so ingeniously that, *through us,* through programs working in our psyche, he is certain to maintain massive influence on corporate and management structures, business processes, and even whole economic systems. These systems in turn will continue to perpetuate his plans; that is, of course, until someone sees through his game plan and thwarts it!

The Devil created a vicious circle in its original sense, and we in particular, the people in business, play a vital – not always very nice – role in the ploy: by creating, recreating and maintaining this vicious circle over and over, through *our* decisions and actions.

Everyone knows the old business quote from the early industrial times: "Business is war". Of course, war still yields the highest rate of return in terms of evil goals: lots of emotional pain, large-scale destruction, the eradication of kindness and respect for other human beings, and as a result, an abundant harvest of destructive emotional energies.

This is important to understand, because, you see, these energies are exactly what the Devil lives on! Negative emotional energies are the Devil's food!

For the Devil, wars are key and politicians or lobbyists who sustain war and bloodshed are the best. The only issue for the Devil with wars is their normally short life-span, as at some stage there always comes a point when people are tired of fighting – or when there are simply no more people left to draft or to kill or there is no further infrastructure to be destroyed.

**So, how then to secure a *constant*, truly long-term and stable energy supply for the Devil?**

In a way this task is quite similar to a strategic management decision, much like in the securities business: potentially higher-yielding, but riskier short-term trading strategies versus less volatile, long-term capital appreciation models. What do you think the Devil chose?

Here is how it all might have been:

> **"What," the Devil may have thought, "if I really could create an effective, long-term source of those emotional qualities I require for a comfortable living – all kinds of fear, anger, continuous feelings of pressure, greed, jealousy and other forms of frustration – but not through short-term wars, rather in the form of a complete self-sustaining *system*?"**

Inasmuch as the Devil is capable of loving, he loved his idea.

> "Returns may not be as high as in a war," he pondered, "but with the help of dogma, large-scale manipulation and working through the human ego and human character weaknesses, I should be able to put a marvellously self-sustaining and stable system in place – hopefully just when God isn't watching."

The more he thought about the idea, the more he got excited.

> "But what should I call that system?" he might have continued to wonder, when all of a sudden he had a fantastic and most creative idea.

> **"Since for such a system to function properly I will have to keep humans constantly under pressure and busy, horribly busy. Why don't I**

**simply call it… a Busy-Ness?... Busi-Ness?... *BUSINESS!*"**

Contemplating his own ingenuity, the Devil laughed an ugly and heartless laugh.

**You see, as the leading dark angel he knew his time would come. He was absolutely certain he would always be cleverer than those God-infested humans, who thought they were so powerful, so incredibly smart. More than that, he felt totally confident that with the human's limited, materialistic and easily manipulated mind they would in fact *never* see through his tricks and manipulations – and work and work, and suffer!**

But will they really?

# 1

# War and peace in business

Our modern corporate and industrial business life often, and quite sadly, seems to resemble hell – and not heaven. Everyone who works in business has experienced it, at one time or another.

Yet this seems so normal to us that we don't even think about it anymore. We don't feel the need to question the meaning of what we do – because we think

"It's only business!" Yes, we have accepted a system that hurts us so thoroughly, as if it were a God-given fact.

Surprise! It is not at all God-given, but "given" from quite the opposite power. Moreover, modern business life is a hell of our own making!

If we break through the mental barriers that the Devil in his ingenuity first installed in our psyches, which then spread throughout our society, through our educational system and our egos, we can quite easily bring more heavenly qualities, like sincere success, powerful joy, fulfilment, inner peace and dignity, back into the business and management world.

**But for the time being and until we begin to help ourselves, "Business is war". How prophetic this quotation from early industrial times has become! This is especially true in a prolonged crisis like the one we are witnessing now.**

**However, for a war you need *enemies*. Someone to fight against. No enemies means no war. Therefore, the Devil had to create a system complete with enemies.**

**We may not like it, nor may we ever have thought about business this way, but the current economic system is *designed* to create enemies. They are created first in our minds, held in place through our belief-system and then manifested in our so-called "business reality".**

You don't believe that?

**In our modern business world there are enemies *everywhere*. Government, yes; competition, particularly yes; and regulators, by all means. These enemies in the outer world in more than one way all threaten our livelihood.**

Of course we also have lots of internal enemies too. Superiors we don't like or who won't promote us, or colleagues who threaten our careers. Very subtly we have to fight them, tactically, unobtrusively, secretly. Even business friends can become enemies, especially when they are highly qualified professionals and want the same top-level job we think should be rightfully ours after all those years of hard work and sacrifice.

What about our own industrial workforce? Enemies? Of course, when it comes to efficiency programs or cost reductions!

**What is top-management fighting against these days? You guessed it. Top management is fighting against costs. And by fighting costs, in 90 per cent of cases, it is fighting against other *human beings*. We tend to overlook that simple but absolutely important fact!**

Moreover, we overlook the possibility that these "other human beings" who are being cut out due to such streamlining can one day be, well, you and me!

**It should be quite clear that in almost all aspects our current business life is characterized by fighting. This fighting does not necessarily have to be an open and aggressive warlike fighting, although even that kind of commercial conflict is sometimes considered chic and macho, especially by our friends in Wall Street. Much rather it is a silent, yet constant, often grim, lonely and desperate fighting – *exactly* as the Devil had wanted and planned it!**

We know it all too well. We are constantly fighting deadlines, we are fighting for revenues, fighting for recognition, fighting for promotion, fighting our competition in the marketplace, fighting for our internal positioning, fighting for profits at the corporate level, fighting against the opinion of others, and in the end, we are forced to fight our own frustration.

This subtle but constant fighting wears us out, a little bit each day. And the more senior in management we are, the more pressure we are under to succeed and the more intensely we have to fight.

**Think about it. Just open the *Financial Times*, the *Wall Street Journal* or the *Handelsblatt* for evidence of this.**

Have we in the modern business world not actually become officers or soldiers without fully recognizing it? Is the system forcing us to engage in a covert, unspoken and silent kind of war, especially as we move up the echelons? A succinct war that we clearly didn't want and for which we were never trained or emotionally prepared?

A fighting that was never our conscious choice; a tactical war which is slowly killing our vision, our motivation, our joy of life and, unless we are very careful, in the end our dignity – and that's not to mention our physical and emotional health.

I know it sounds provocative, but if you think logically you will realize that no being with any wisdom, respect for humankind or emotional intelligence would ever set a system up this way.

So, who then did set it up and whose energy fuels it?

The funny and scary part is that we ourselves maintain, live and work in this system every single day.

Of course there are smart ways out, and we will look at those together in the second half of the book.

For now, however, it is a question of understanding. Let's take a short look at Darwinism. Survival of the fittest, the others must perish...Darwin's teaching did not exactly bring many positive impulses to the world. His ideas were snapped up by dictators such as Stalin and Hitler and (one cannot help but have the impression) even by some modern political leaders.

**A tragedy, we say. In business we are different. We know better, we have our mission statements, believe in fairness, in the worth of our human assets and we foster teamwork. But let us be frank. What philosophy do we in business *really* still believe in?**

Think about this with complete honesty for a moment.

I fully realize that these words are not particularly pleasant to hear, but better read or hear them now, while you have time to reflect upon them – and while you can still change something, if you want to.

Sadly the current economic crisis only exacerbates those war-like pressures. Who isn't fighting costs fervently? Just look at all those ingenious corporate streamlining programs.

The real tragedy, though, with any aggressive form of fighting is the fact that there are so many injuries, both open and hidden; painful emotional wounds, that sometimes take many years to heal. Could that be the reason why in management you see so many tense, pressured and stressed people, fighting their way through life? Fighting, because they don't know any better?

Not such a happy affair, is it?

Whether we like it or not, the Devil always was and still is utterly ingenious and extremely efficient. He lures us into a business world that is driven largely by promises, an often futile search for "security", and a predominantly ego-driven need for recognition and by widespread materialism. He lures us into a world that in most cases doesn't do us that much good, a world that so often causes us pain. Lots of unseen, but deeply seated and ultimately destructive emotional pain.

I do know what I am talking about.

Following thousands of often very delicate and personal conversations with senior executives in corporate businesses around the world, you cannot turn a blind eye anymore. I have seen the emotional pain and I have seen its destructive effects again and again.

Yet what is our standard response in business?

With seeming effectiveness we paint over it. Painting over it makes us look strong and professional, but is has one catch: it is not honest. The human mind is clever. It can betray others and it can even betray itself, actually for a very long time. But not forever.

You may have heard the saying: "When we are young we run after money with our health, but once we're over the hill we run after health with our money."

Not very intelligent of us, is it? But look around you: it seems everybody is doing it that way.

A friend of mine, a well-known and reputable business psychologist, said to me earnestly when we talked about this subject: "Look, maybe it's already too late for you. Part of your life is gone, and gone forever. But your unfulfilled aspirations, your disillusionment and your health problems, they are all still here. Do not let those be your heritage." That moment was a big turning point in my life, when I realized how right he was. I had ignored it all in my fight for positioning and success.

That conversation took place when I was 44. And I decided to take action. This book is one of the results of that decision.

As I said, the Devil is not nice, but efficient. He needs those weakened souls, those exhausted people. You see, they are easier to harvest than strong and joy-filled souls.

And what about God? Couldn't God have slapped the Devil's hand and put him in his place?

The fact is that God didn't! At least that's how it seems. But why?

Because this is a planet of free will and none but ourselves are in charge of our own destiny.

Ahh, the Devil is mighty, I hear you say. How true. But then I also hear you say, the Devil may be mighty, but God is *al*mighty!

Great, but you see that may not be completely true. In a hand closed as a fist not even an almighty God can put all his goodies. That is how powerful human free will *really* is. And that is how big our responsibility for our own life has become.

Bear with me on this philosophical level for just one more moment – it is important – before we become practical and talk about solutions. Let us explore a hypothetical example: if you are God setting up a planet of freewill, all you can do logically is to provide a framework of reference and plant in the consciousness of the inhabitants the wisdom of how all problems can be solved. But you cannot take decisions for the inhabitants. If you did that you would kill their freewill and their chance of development, something you would never do because you love and respect the inhabitants, your own creation.

On a planet of freewill the inhabitants have to take individual and specific decisions themselves. This is how they grow, how they can become self-conscious and ultimately successful.

In order to help us along, occasionally God can send a messenger, an enlightened being, one who peacefully reminds us of God's original ways, the ways of respect, kindness and dignity. The way of true human intelligence.

Over the millennia he probably sent quite a number. However, these radiant beings are rarely "mainstream", and the mainstream didn't want to hear their messages.

How then did we, us human beings here on earth, with frightening regularity, react to those messengers? We killed them – or at least ridiculed them.

This is how it is with us humans.

So there we are, back to square one.

Putting it metaphorically, we cannot blame the Devil for trying to hurt and seduce us. And we cannot blame God for creating a sphere of freewill.

Either God is serious about it and gives us real freewill or this whole game of life is possibly just a charade.

Pretty serious stuff, isn't it? It is most relevant for understanding what we really do in business, but I bet they didn't teach you that at business school.

Whichever way you look at it, in the end we are back to ourselves, because that is all we have. All the way back to the choices we make.

**Why is all this so relevant? Because of *you*, dear reader!**

**Remember this most important fact: in the way that this is all set up, the Devil has *no* power at all! There is no fight between God and the Devil. The fight is between the Devil and *us*! And business life gives us ample opportunities to decide where we stand with our decisions.**

The Devil gets his life-energy from one source exclusively, and that is from us humans. This is his one and only source! And unless we change it, this will continue to be a good and rich source.

Can we change it? Here's the good news: Yes, we can! And together we will explore how that can be done.

Let us conclude here by remembering that, in a way, looking at it soberly, we can leave God out for a moment. He simply created the possibilities. The actual theatre of operation, where decisions between good and bad, honesty or manipulation, kindness or aggressiveness are made and manifested, is right here, within you and me.

Let that sink in before we move on to look at the Devil's profit motives.

# 2 What the Devil gets out of it

What does the Devil get out of the immense game we call business?

Interesting question? One that is not too often asked, I would guess.

Before we dig any further, I would like to make it clear that we are largely speaking in symbolic language here. At a conceptual level the story is set against the philosophical background of heaven and hell, good and bad, God and the Devil.

The terms God and the Devil, good and evil, heaven and hell are therefore used metaphorically and are not meant to be interpreted in any religious sense. Particularly so because every established religion seems to have its own claim, or rather "beneficial ownership", of good and evil.

We shall be good citizens and not invade already occupied territory. After all, we don't want to start yet another religious war by disputing who exactly now has the monopoly on God (and with that, the monopoly on evil!).

But if you want my opinion on this subject, here it is:

**The vast creative energy we call or imagine as "God" existed a very long time before this galaxy came into being and before the first human beings started to develop on this little planet of ours. I personally don't buy the idea of organizations being smart or holy enough to put such an immense and universal energy into a little box called "religion", which organizations then try to monopolize and sell to often gullible human beings as the only truth. It's good business, and remember who created it!**

**Of course all these organizations claim that *their* religion "comes directly from God". But can they prove that?**

Of course not! All religions come from and through human beings. If any particular religion did come directly from God, then only that one religion speaks the truth, and all other religions would have to be regarded as impostors. By claiming their special status each one of those organized religions creates confusion and competition. And with it they sow the seeds of fighting for superiority, which in a way is insane or at least immensely arrogant, since all religions claim to be based on the same principles, the principles of peace and of love. Because, at least on paper, this is every religion's declared goal.

**Now show me any Western organized religion that is *truly* generous, thoroughly peaceful, completely honest,**

**filled with love and which never uses force, fear or pressure in arguments. Although most organized religions claim that they are living these values, the only religion I can think of that is truly peaceful and thoroughly honest is Buddhism.**

The following is an example from my own business life that demonstrates this point:

In addition to being the CEO, I operationally ran the Financial Services Practice Group of our executive search firm due to my background in investment banking. One day I received a business call from a rather unusual gentleman, a Benedictine monk. I shall call him Brother Martin.

It turned out that Brother Martin was the head of administration of a large and famous Benedictine monastery. It was famous not only for its architectural beauty, its treasures of art and paintings, but equally for the quality of wine it produced and exported. I didn't know it then, but this monastery, which is almost 1,000 years old, is also one of the most important landlords in the whole region, owning everything from farms to apartment buildings. For one reason or another I had been recommended to Brother Martin as a professional with the right connections in the financial services industry.

Before I continue I'd like to recount the political setting of this conversation. It took place in 1999. The Kosovo war in former Yugoslavia with all its atrocities had just ended and the Catholic Church had started a special nationwide collection program. During each mass Catholics were asked to contribute as much as possible in order to help refugees in Kosovo. "Even if it is just a couple of small coins," the Church said in emotional messages that appealed to our compassion. I vaguely remember that this program brought in several millions, making it quite a success. Even the Head of Caritas thanked the population for its generosity.

Back to the business request:

Our potential client told me on the phone that his monastery had had an operational review and that they wanted to improve and professionalize their internal organization, which included their asset management. They were looking for one, possibly two, professional asset managers, ideally with solid banking backgrounds. If I felt up to the task and if the fee suggested by us was reasonable he would proceed to send me a job description the monastery had prepared. It went without saying that this search would have to be conducted in a highly confidential manner – i.e. we would not be allowed to divulge the identity of our client until our client had seen and evaluated each potential final candidate's CV.

The confidentiality rules were not unusual and were acceptable to us. However, I told him that before I could indicate a fee, I really had to see the job description. Its content would decide the level of complexity, search radius and resources required in order to identify and attract candidates with the right kind of experience. He hesitated but I finally managed to persuade him to let me have the job description first.

Brother Martin sent it by fax and after I had read it I understood his concern for confidentiality. Since I had promised that, I cannot go into any details here, but I can say as much: the ideal candidate would have to have several years of money market, FX and other related trading experience. He (the candidate had to be male) would also need to document detailed knowledge of investment strategies and ideally have a professional track record in financial asset management, covering bonds, money market instruments, options and other derivatives. The person would also be asked to provide advice on dealing with the revenue stream from the monastery's rental income.

Last but not least the job description gave an indication, although without specific numbers, of trading and exposure volumes the person would have to be capable of dealing with. From these figures it was easy to guess the asset values, a large part of which were in liquid assets, our potential candidate would have to manage. The funds were, to put it mildly, substantial!

**I was speechless, and for a moment I wasn't sure if I should laugh or cry. Conservatively estimated, just the liquid part of the net assets (or funds "under management") of this single monastery would have fed *all* refugees in Kosovo for the next 100 years!**

**What would *you* do in such a situation?**

On the one hand the assignment itself was quite demanding of us; on the other hand, the monastery was prepared to pay us market rates and a substantial performance-related bonus to the candidate. In terms of career and CV development it would be difficult to get good people from the banking industry to move to a monastery. So all in all it would turn out to be quite a challenging project.

But there were other criteria to consider. Officially asking citizens to donate money, “even if it’s just some coins”, while at the same time sitting on such substantial funds which were to be professionally managed, reminded me of the own-trading departments of investment banks, and the identity of motives: maximize profit and increase the asset base. It just didn’t match. And in that single moment it all felt phoney to me.

But sometimes synchronicity helps us to make decisions. Next morning I found a not too friendly letter from the local diocese, claiming that this year I should pay a higher church tax assessment because my income was higher compared to the previous year.

Of course I could have taken on this assignment and used my share of the proceeds to pay the higher church tax, but I didn’t.

I sent Brother Martin a friendly e-mail, declining the opportunity. I guess he already knew why, because he didn’t even ask for the reason. His only concern was that we dispose of the job description and keep the contents confidential.

Let’s get back to the main theme.

Once you realize how rigid, often hypocritical and therefore damaging old religious belief systems can be, you cannot help but become quite critical.

Here, I am not talking about the often lovely priests and other selfless guys – and girls, such as Catholic nuns – in the field, God’s local sales reps, who do all the caring work. I’m talking about the hierarchy people who manage and run those organizations. Many of these people have no choice, at least in their minds, but to use power tactics and manipulation to get to the top and to stay "in power". There are probably numerous examples familiar to us. These people are almost certainly no closer to God than any one of us.

I know I may sound rather harsh, and you may also wonder why, in a business book, there is a whole chapter about such topics. This is because the correlation between what you believe in and how your world is subsequently constructed in your mind is extremely high, and because issues of good and bad, God and the Devil, massively, but normally sub-consciously, influence your behaviour and your thinking, especially about business.

Read on and you'll see how that works!

We are much stronger than we think! After years of observation and dealing with the human character, I can say that we are smart ourselves and we can think critically. We all have a heart, an open mind, we can love and we have deep feelings. Our goodness is a natural part of us. We are already well equipped to liberate ourselves.

**As a result every intelligent human being has the right, and in my opinion the full moral obligation to himself or herself, to develop *their own* view of God and the Devil. These deep and important questions are always personal regardless, whereas all organized religious beliefs, due to their hierarchies, become stiff and dogmatic, and therefore impersonal. Also their views are, in the final analysis, purely subjective. These religions are just interpretations, nothing else. Any organized religion is only an individual opinion – and should be recognized precisely as such. As an *opinion*!**

And as we know, opinions can be right or wrong. Or, as Mark Twain wrote: "Whenever you find yourself on the side of the majority, it's high time to pause and reflect."

But the moment we start to argue and fight about who is right and who is wrong, we only serve one specific energy, and that energy is clearly not God.

**Yet that is precisely what we do most or even all of the time, in our religious beliefs as much as in business. We fight and by fighting we hurt ourselves and others, causing a lot of emotional pain, and that, dear reader, is exactly *what the Devil gets out of it.***

# 3

# Early choices and "trying to make it"

How, then, did we get ourselves into this mess?

**Remember, the choices *we* make determine if our life moves closer to heavenly or hellish circumstances. This is especially true in all areas of business and management. The question is, do we actually have that many choices?**

Yes, we do – and more than we think, or are made to believe we have.

But let us start by analysing under what circumstances, and indeed at what point in time in our life, do we make those destiny-influencing career choices, such as studying for an MBA, becoming a lawyer or going into business.

We do it, or rather, we are forced to do it, much too early!

**Who told you that choosing a career in business would be a good option for you? Or indeed that it**

**would the *right* choice? Did you really know that for yourself or did society possibly create a mental image which you then followed? Think back to when you were a lad or girl of 18 or 19 years. Were you fully aware of your strengths, weaknesses, your desires, your capabilities or your character? Or were you, like pretty much every teenager, filled with high hopes but equally full of good-willed illusions, mainly about yourself and the (business) world?**

If you talk in depth to thousands of business executives (which is something as the Regional CEO of a global executive search firm I had to do and still do today), and if you don't merely focus on business credentials but instead look at each executive's personality, their character, their personal reality and their hopes and frustrations, you are confronted with a rather surprising fact. A fact that hardly ever gets published in business books or magazines!

The vast majority of those people who opted for a business career – and spent their entire adult life "making it" or at least trying to do so – had no idea what they had let themselves in for!

I can speak definitely about senior business executives, as they were my focus, but I'm convinced that the same would apply at all layers of management.

**If we turn to hard figures, less than 30 per cent (!) of the business executives I encountered, worked with, interviewed or audited, were *certain* that the corporate function, the line of business they were in or the industry they worked for, was truly the right one for them. "Right" in the sense that it suited their talent structure, emotional make-up or personal vision of themselves.**

Why such a low number? Because when they first took those destiny-making decisions, or even later in their business life, few of them ever asked themselves these three key questions:

- **Does the work I do truly suit my talents and character?**
- **Does it match my personal vision of how I want to live?**
- **Does it make me happy?**

In those conversations with senior executives I could clearly see that their reasons for following a business career – be it in banking, industry, professional services, you name it – were that they had been promised three things: success, money and prestige – and lots of it!

**There was just one tiny, tiny catch to it all, the small print in the soul contract, if you like: these wonderful outcomes could all be yours, provided you were willing to sacrifice...well, *something*.**

You see, the Devil is smart and remarkably efficient.

So what was it that you were expected to sacrifice? (And in most cases, you even offered to do so willingly.) In order to answer this, let us observe the reality of corporate life.

How many of you actually got all the success, the corporate positioning, the money and prestige – and remember you wanted lots of it – that you had hoped and worked (or shall we say, bargained) for?

Not that easy to answer, is it?

Could it be that the system is actually designed to lead us into temptation, and that we accept that as a given?

Could it be that the system plays with our ever-so-slightly corruptible and greedy egos, because our egos are easy to manipulate?

Could it be that the system actually doesn't care about us? Could it be that we asked the wrong authority when it came to planning our lives?

Critical questions indeed.

So, returning to the original issue: what were we expected (and which we willingly offered) to sacrifice?

How about: the quality of our lives?

Isn't it true that most of us have sacrificed inner peace and a more natural lifestyle in exchange for an immensely stress-ridden lifestyle, a lifestyle that leaves hardly any time to look for the true meaning of our lives?

It's not only in senior management, but in all echelons of the business world that we have been forced to sacrifice aspects of our dignity. Even worse, the system has persuaded us to accept and believe in those ever-so-slightly corrupt values at some stage.

In the meantime, where did the values that were once so important to us that we taught them to our children as guidelines for life – values such as fairness, honesty, integrity and compassion – go?

But that's not all.

In far too many cases, we sacrificed our health as well. It's too bad that we don't get many second chances when it comes to our health.

**Isn't it somewhat strange, upon reflection, that it is precisely these values (inner peace, dignity, health, kindness and happiness) that we naturally associate with heaven? And that they are the values which *every* human being in *every* culture truly seeks, yet in our business world you hardly ever find them?**

There is such a discrepancy between the business system and what humans truly need.

**I have met so many wonderful people in management and business. Intelligent people, people with a heart. It makes me sad to see their problems, to feel their frustration. It has to do with the fact that they do not dare ask critical questions about their place in the system or about the validity of the system itself. To all of them I say: "Be careful not to forget about *yourself* in all your activity." And I sincerely mean this!**

Since we are essentially good-natured, we tend to give our best. Maybe, as a friend recently remarked sarcastically, it would be smarter to keep our best for ourselves!

Continuing with that thought, would it not be logical that a metaphorical God loves his children, whereas the metaphorical Devil does not?

It is therefore only logical to conclude that creating an environment that produces happiness is what God would want, whereas sustaining an environment that produces unhappiness, fear and emotional frustration is what the Devil wants.

What is the solution?

**Here it is: remember free will – *your* free will. Use this tremendously powerful gift!**

Free will is really the start. Recognizing what the Devil wants is the next step, followed by an understanding of how he gets it.

# 4 Business traps

True to his devious philosophies, the Devil works through traps.

However, if you observe the business world with a certain inner distance, you cannot escape the impression that its denizens are strangely fond of their daily share of stress, unhappiness and frustration.

If your workplace makes you unhappy for a substantial portion of your (life)-time – a very real problem as shown in a recent report released by the US Conference Board entitled: "US job satisfaction at lowest level in two decades" – why are we not actively, and with determination, looking for something better?

If you are ill you try to escape that through taking medicine. If you step into a swarm of bees you run as fast as you can. In normal life we swiftly get out of painful circumstances. It's our natural response.

But what about in business?

We stay, we suffer, we might have a little success here and there, we get frustrated, we become a little complacent, and we get scared and find a thousand reasons for not getting off our backsides.

Since we are not entirely stupid, let alone masochistic, there must be a catch to this somewhere. There must be a trap.

**And indeed there is. The following are summaries of five *open* and *hidden* business traps that the Devil has planted in order to keep us subdued.**

## Trap No. 1: Commercial pressures – the quintessential *open* catch

Being constantly driven by fear – and remember, this is the Devil's favourite tool in creating and maintaining business pressure – we find numerous excuses for not taking action. The new job may not be any better; we could even be financially worse off; changing jobs may create unforeseen risks; there may not even be a better job out there, etc.

**Is that really all there is to life, *your* life, all it is offered by the business world? Do we say to our children after years of college or university: My child, life is so dangerous, be pessimistic and use your MBA to find a secure place, perhaps at the Post Office?**

**You smile…we don't want to destroy the vitality and enthusiasm of our children, do we? But someone has possibly destroyed *ours*.**

And what do we, the so-called adults, actually tell our children, our family, ourselves and society, if we remain in business or management positions that are unfulfilling, if we hold onto jobs that have no more meaning except (hopefully!) that they secure us a certain cash-flow? What do we truly say to the world around us if they can all feel the discontent, recognize the frustration and see how exhausted we have become?

We might mutter to ourselves: "Suffer, shut up and perform; don't ask for meaning; and don't expect kindness and fulfilment".

Is that what we really wanted for ourselves – or want today for our friends, our families or for the next generation? Is that the vision we should continue to perpetuate to others through the example we set? Is that what we have let business turn us into?

Have we sold ourselves and, if so, at what price? Is our life and happiness really worth so little that we have sacrificed the beautiful gift of a fulfilled life and a balanced soul on the altar of commercial success, which itself is often ill-defined?

Whom do we serve by living in such a way?

Remember, actions speak louder than words, and if you are resigned to this way of life, what a sad example you must be setting for those around you.

## Trap No 2: The "ifs of business life" – the ultimate in self-betrayal

***If* top-management changes its strategy or *if* we can change the company culture, then things will surely get better; *if* I make it to another seven years, I will have**

**my peace in retirement; (and now the worst one of all:) *if* we reach our budget, the pressure will decrease.**

**How many of the above *if's* has ever happened and miraculously changed your working life? When has reaching your budget ever decreased performance pressure?**

I think you know the answer.

Who is to blame?

This is the Devil's ultimate but semi-hidden trap of *self-betrayal.*

## Trap No. 3: Limited (self)-awareness – a usually well-hidden, but utterly treacherous trap

**Why don't we move away from those jobs and positions that make us unhappy? Because to do so, we have to believe we *can* – and that we *should* – move. In other words, we must have the mental, intellectual and emotional freedom – a well developed level of self-awareness – to envisage the world as a place full of opportunities, in which we deserve to lead a more fulfilled business life. This is a life that is ultimately meant to be good.**

Yet what is our existing business and management culture, especially our media, and most of our organised religions, teaching us? Exactly the opposite!

**Let's assume we want to live an intelligent and worthy life. By simply reflecting on the core values noted down in, say, our constitution (freewill, dignity,**

**the right of self-expression), we all of a sudden realize that society, the media and business as they are currently constructed does everything to *prevent* us from achieving that goal.**

You only have to watch the news (another mighty tool of the Devil) to see how they nail you down in cynicism and negativity, and systematically destroy your belief in the goodness of your fellow man, and your positive and constructive approach to life.

Could it be that there is a truly nasty system at work here, a hidden and intricate system that the average person regards as "normal", but which in fact has no regard for true human values, despite constant and loud claims to the opposite?

A system, furthermore, that abhors people who want to think their own thoughts, especially thoughts about business?

A society which wants to keep us under its thumb is the prime reason why it is hard to escape from an – at best – average life, a business life with little meaning and often referred to as "mainstream".

The current business world is often a heartless system operating through a thoughtless society, but portrayed as a "caring society", even if that lie can be seen by all intelligent people.

Remember, the Devil is extremely smart and he is devious beyond human imagination.

If a lie is repeated a thousand times, most people will buy into it, but it is still nevertheless a lie.

## Trap No. 4: Responsibilities – (most of them falsely understood).

This is the hardest trap to avoid because it is so overloaded with emotions – of shame, of self- importance, of failure, of sacrifice – and where emotions fly high, reason cannot prevail.

Before we go further, we need to differentiate the kinds of responsibilities we are faced with in our business lives:

- Business responsibilities that are loaded onto us from outside, and
- Personal responsibilities that we sincerely feel in our hearts

For the sake of clarity, personal responsibilities for other human beings that we feel in our hearts, and which come from our true inner being, from the goodness we carry within ourselves, should always be taken seriously.

But in daily commercial reality these form only a minor part of our overall responsibilities.

What hurts people's lives and their integrity is business responsibilities we so often accept without criticism, or accept because we are told to do so. These are business responsibilities that come down on us like the Ten Commandments.

And just as it is with the Ten Commandments, it is politically incorrect even to question them a little.

All of these responsibilities, often forced upon us, that come from outside, from above, from the board, from all kinds of hierarchies, should be critically questioned, even challenged, if our own lives are to continue to have meaning for ourselves.

We are often reminded that looking critically at "responsibilities", even actively rejecting some of them, goes against the grain of our social culture and work ethic. But this is not true, as you will see in a moment.

Those who want to prevent us from being critical of such externally sourced "responsibilities" want us to be without options, want us to perform and not ask questions. They literally want us to be without a response-ability! It's the same system found in the military or in politics, and which is presently applied to business.

Here are three (perhaps rather exaggerated) examples for illustrative purposes.

Imagine if during a strategic board meeting all of sudden a discussion is started, not about sales, share values or organizational goals, but around "true ethical values". Is it morally, ethically and humanly right in the way we organize ourselves? Is it right to do what we do commercially? Just imagine such questions and discussions taking place during the board meeting of an arms manufacturers or a company which pollutes the environment…

Imagine if a senior army officer starts taking ethics seriously. He begins to question the justification for hurting and killing other people, often civilians, in foreign countries; people who for political reasons have been declared "enemies" by our politicians, the same politicians who, of course, would never allow their own children to come near to real danger.

And wouldn't it be an even worst horror scenario if constituents demanded that their governments stop mortgaging theirs, and their children's and their grandchildren's lives with debt burdens that will have to be paid by the citizens, and certainly not by the government or the irresponsible politicians who incurred that debt.

**Remember the title of this book. Remember who created this culture and this system, created these work ethics and who profits from them and wants to sustain them. A system that may have been noble at some stage, long in the past, a system that is so degenerate that, especially nowadays in times of crisis, it can only survive if it continuously exploits and takes advantage of others. It is a system that can sustain itself only by using up others' life-energy – or more precisely and sadly, *your* life-energy.**

You see, with that little word "responsibility" you can dress up a lot and manipulate even more. You can nicely embellish the concept and then with "responsibility" you can demand almost any injustice or immoral or unethical behaviour, in politics – but equally in business.

**This trap, however, is particularly destructive: for by cleverly using the "responsibility trap", the system can turn our hurtful behaviour even against *ourselves.***

Sounds really tough and unpleasant, doesn't it? But for a moment take a critical look at reality and think for yourself.

When did you last talk to your boss or your board about the moral righteousness of what your firm produces or sells? Were you encouraged to address this issue or were you swiftly asked to change your focus, because bringing up such an issue could threaten the company's operations and its profits, and might cause redundancies (including your own)?

Did you ever ask this crucial question?

"Yes, I did," I hear you say, "it was when we last discussed our mission statement and the new PR campaign on how our company was to be positioned in the marketplace" Ouch. Try again!

## Trap No. 5: The most insidious and dangerous of them all!

It took me many years to discover and then even more years to understand fully this one. It's almost impossible to detect, also difficult to describe, but I'll try nevertheless.

It started with the original issue of why so many people in business are frustrated with what they do and therefore are unhappy, and yet why they are so passive in taking steps to change their situation.

The reason is a delicate and well-hidden vicious circle. In fact it is so well hidden in our psyche that our chance of detecting it within ourselves is small.

This trap is called: addiction!

**Why do we *not* stop drinking when we rationally already know that we have had enough, that it can damage our health or lead us into dangerous situations? Why can't we stop eating heavy dinners even when we feel bad the next day each time? Why do people who are taking daily doses of pills or drugs**

**still deny that they are dependent on them? Why are people in business, who are working at physical or emotional stress levels that are clearly injurious, unable to stop, even though they are highly intelligent and should know better?**

The answer is: it's an addiction. An addiction that runs in an insidious upward circle that goes like this: hard work – hoped-for reward – exhaustive work and more responsibility as the reward – creating more stress – even more reward and responsibilities required to make up for all that sacrifice – leading to higher self-inflicted distress and accepted pressure – to be compensated for by even more rewards to balance and make you forget the stress – and so on.

It is the result of a falsely understood system of "rewards", which we in our thinking accept as normal, although the whole process goes against our true nature and is counter-intuitive.

**This is not meant to belittle the importance of work, even of working hard, but through the appreciation we seek or the money we want to get for the pain we are willing to bear, we reward ourselves in a most unhealthy way. Sometimes we are even proud of it (we bear the dangerous stress level "like a man") and forget that it was we *ourselves* who induced that stress-level in the first place.**

By tying ourselves to this reward-stress-reward-punishment machine, we inflict damage on ourselves. And it is only we ourselves who can unwind that process.

Apart from your doctor and possibly your small children, who still have that natural kind of innocent intelligence, has anybody cared to warn you about what you are doing to yourself? Probably not.

The reason is that this self-inflicted damage is exactly what the system wants you to do. It is playing a nasty game with your ego. We could say, no. But we don't. And because it is a form of addiction, we have a hard time admitting it to ourselves.

I know exactly what I'm talking about, because I myself did it for many years. I suffered from and complained about the inhuman levels of stress in business, then vigorously jumped in again the next day. I needed the emotional kick. It took me years to understand that I was addicted to stress. Stress gave me the feeling of importance. Sometimes my overblown ego even found something heroic in this daily struggle. But in reality it catered to the most primitive level of emotion, made me ill and cost me my marriage.

The treacherous thing about this kind of addiction is that as the stress-level increases, your need to compensate for it with all kinds of rewards increases as well, and the positive emotional increment of rewarding yourself takes a downward path.

In effect, your need for daily doses (in this case, stress and rewards) gets increasingly higher, while the perception of what you are actually doing to yourself and your life become increasingly obscured.

This is not so different from alcoholics or serious drug addicts.

Look at how executives brag about their ever increasing stress-levels, as if that made them nobler. It doesn't. If anything it makes it clear to everyone observing them that they are not in charge any more and have actually lost control over their lives.

Then one day your wife says she's had enough, and that you love your stress more than you love her or your family. She is totally right. But do we want to admit it?

You see, the Devil is utterly devious in the expert way in which he plays with our egos.

**It should now be clear how we get caught and drawn into hurting ourselves by the Devil in business: by appealing *not* to our natural intelligence, but to our ego.**

Perhaps further proof of this is a saying which has been widely accepted, yet is one of the least intelligent sayings our upside-down social and business world has ever produced. You have all heard it many times: "Work hard, play hard".

**Essentially a person who believes in this is saying: "My ego needs stress *all* the time! I've become such a self-destructive addict that even my rewards should come from a stressful environment." Moreover, "I'm so totally out of balance that I stopped caring for my own life." Ultimately it saying: "I haven't really understood that great gift called human existence."**

Sometimes one cannot help but to admire the Devil for his ingenuity and manipulative powers. Making us in business do such damage to ourselves is in itself a remarkable achievement, but creating a whole human society that inadvertently – or may be even consciously, who knows – promotes "values" that systematically damage the human being, is a pure masterpiece.

Too bad we now have to call the Devil's bluff.

By now, one or even all five business traps invented by the Devil may be familiar to you, and you recognize that they are all there in your own life.

If that is the case: beautiful! It's time to look them in the eye. Maybe you have discovered more traps than the five above. Even better!

At first it maybe easier to see how others have fallen into those traps before you recognize them in your own life. The process is not easy.

**But we are concerned about individual meaning and *your* happiness. So you have to work for it, because nobody else will do it for you.**

Remember, the Devil's traps are just traps, nothing more. It's quite possible to avoid them because a trap you recognize is one that has largely lost its threat. Use your intelligence and your courage to stay clear of them from now on. You really owe that to yourself!

Let me conclude this chapter with a parable.

When the Pilgrim Fathers set out to leave England behind in 1620, they would most probably have been told that their ideas of freedom were an illusion and a threat to Royal society, that they had a moral responsibility to the King, a responsibility to stay and to work hard for the Crown.

These wise and respected men might have answered: "With all due respect, Sire, we see our responsibilities in a different light. We are intelligent enough to think, and decide, for ourselves what is good for us – and what is not! We want to have the freedom to feel and decide our destiny in our own hearts, and to be the masters of our lives. But rest assured, Sire, you need not worry – many souls are still here, serving diligently but probably thoughtlessly your own well-being."

# 5

# Common ending

When you enter business life as a young investment banker, coming directly from Harvard Business School as I did, you are filled with mental pictures of what business is all about and how it works and with emotional concepts that later will lay the foundations of your motivational structures.

You aspire to "make it", as you have been rigorously trained to do, in order to fulfil your dreams. Dreams of prestige, money and buying all those things that represent "the good life". Then there's the pursuit of power. Again and again, it's portrayed by the media and business school that those with power have a better life; they have it easier; they are the real winners.

We enter business life much like a private in the army, there is a chain of command, in which a senior officer constantly maintains both emotional pressure and emotional promise. As a result you invest all you have – your time, your energy, your creativity, all your acquired knowledge and your intellectual acumen – in pursuing a winner-image of yourself.

You never dare to consider the likelihood of ending up as a loser, although your intelligence could already tell you early on that the odds of making it to the top in virtually any medium-sized company are about 10,000 to 1. Those are indeed heavy odds stacked against you.

Even if you were smart enough to realize this, your ego wouldn't let you off the hook. Your chances of "making it" remain intact, so go for it, young man! The shame of not having made it is too great to bear, too hard to contemplate, and so you spend the early part of your working life neglecting the "not making it to the top" option.

At some stage, however, you begin to realize the hidden cost to this immense struggle. Your social life becomes increasingly superficial. It may also cost you real friendships because you simply don't have time anymore.

It very often causes you to act without regard for others, especially as you approach the top of the corporate hierarchy. This usually makes you sad, but it's something you can't admit to yourself, because some of those "others" have become friends over time. Indeed all friendship usually ends when both or more of you compete for the same managerial position.

This constant struggle and the effort associated with it in the early period of your career when you are young will sadly cost you the quality of your life during a time when your life should be at its most meaningful.

I have seen it happen much too often: businesspeople in their early forties, sometimes even before that, unconsciously begin to "redimension" their business and ethical values, usually due to the relentless business pressures they are under.

> "It is one of those moments," as one of the more open executives I discussed this topic with once said, "when you think back to business school, and all of a sudden you remember your professor's ambivalence, when he talked about business ethics – and now, years later, you understand."

And if that were not enough, the relentless struggle can cost you something that once lost, is almost impossible to regain in your life: your innocence or what some call integrity.

It is therefore no wonder that there are so few real winners in business life. The system seems to be designed that way.

**And who in the end pays for your frustration once you realize you're probably *never* going to make it "to the top"? After you have worked 20 years only to end up in a position two levels below the board?**

**Well, *you* pay for it!**

**Without feeling any shame for its treachery, the same system that lured you with promises and appeals to your ego, will cynically tell you that it was *you* who made the mistake; it was *you* who fell for an illusion, an illusion of your own grandeur and importance.**

When this happens we tend to somehow rationalize it away, and indeed, this is most understandable. We tell ourselves it was "still a good career", and look with compassion upon those others who didn't even make it to our level in the hierarchy.

But in those lonely evenings we know that we cannot cheat our intuitive feelings: we gave a lot, but we may have made a mistake in accepting without criticism a business system that cannot survive unless it produces many losers.

We come to realize that we have given away our power to a corporate institution that does not, and cannot, have feelings for us. We worked hard and accepted sacrifice for a system that doesn't care for us and will never understand what we need. We come to realize that we stopped being masters of our lives, when it would still have been possible to change track.

Such recognition is tough and it hits you hard, irrespective of whether you are 33 or 55 years of age.

This observation applies to all levels of management in the corporate world, even to the top echelons/CEOs. I have seen and met many of these burned out managers, many of whom are rich but empty, some are ill, who are afraid of what will happen when they fall into the void of a no-more-executive existence.

In order for you to avoid this fate I suggest you remember these three key questions, and for the sake of the quality of your own life, ask them frequently:

- **Does the work I do truly suit my talents and character?**
- **Does it match my personal vision of how I want to live?**
- **Does it make me happy?**

In this context I would like to tell you about a business event that in many ways says it all.

A few years ago I was asked to help identify and select a top level Marketing Director for the "Diet Drink" division for the Central and Eastern European business of one of the global market leaders in soft drinks. With three-figure revenues, the region covered 17 countries, and was one of the most promising growth regions for our client.

The two finalists – a 44-year-old male and a 39-year-old female – were experienced and senior professionals who were quite similar in terms of their skill set and background. For a number of reasons I tended towards the female candidate, as I felt that her personality was slightly more appropriate. The corporate culture of our client was rather aggressive and she seemed to have more bite than the male candidate.

I was not disappointed: she had built a truly impressive career, despite a divorce and the fact that she had remained a single mother. Raising a 14-year-old daughter was no problem at all for her. In the course of our discussions we touched upon all sorts of topics: marketing strategies, target group identification processes (especially in the emerging CEE markets), implementation of these strategies, brand positioning and so on.

At some stage she started to describe in detail her strategies for winning over Eastern European teenagers as the prime target group for "Diet Drinks". This lady was smart; her concepts had substance.

> "Teenies," she said, "are often so naive, indeed so vain that catching them with status messages and some 'emotional kick' arguments is not really that difficult." She was right – and her market-related success proved it.

To this day I still do not know what, all of a sudden, prompted me to ask a question that had the effect of an emotional splinter-bomb:

> "Would you also have your 14-year-old daughter consume those diet products you market so aggressively?"
>
> "Of course not," was her snap answer, which probably surprised herself as much as it did me.

Then she hesitated, as if she wanted to apologize. For a second she looked embarrassed but quickly regained her composure. She was a professional, after all. Maybe the surprised expression on my face triggered something which in her mind prompted a justification – which flew at me a split of a second later.

She forcefully insisted she was a professional and an executive, and being paid damned well for reaching targets and for executing business plans. Judging what was good or bad, healthy or unhealthy for the consumer was not part of her job description.

But it did not sound authentic.

I probed the wound. I replied that I had read that artificial sweeteners used in soft drinks had drastically negative side-effects, obesity and other addictive effects, and that my then partner, an experienced doctor, had advised me and my kids not to consume what she called "unhealthy chemical cocktails in soft drinks". By the same token I continued to assure her that under no circumstance was I trying to belittle her impressive business success and track record.

Until that moment she had been full of drive, clarity and, in a pleasant way, self-assurance, but the facial expression of the lady had changed once I uttered that sentence.

Now she seemed stressed and all of a sudden insecure.

I kept quiet, in order to give her time to collect herself, time to find a professional re-entry point into our discussion. Of course, professionally, I was interested in seeing how she would behave under such emotional pressure and how she would deal with a situation that was clearly difficult and delicate for her.

It turned out she had totally misinterpreted my silence.

In a quiet voice that could only be described as somewhere between serious and pained, yet now fully authentic, she answered:

> "You have no idea how exactly this issue worries me every single day in my job!"
>
> "Of course the guys in R&D and in the laboratories all know exactly what the drinks do – and I know it as well. That is the reason why I do not want my daughter to drink that stuff. Every day I could bring home a six-pack if I wanted to, but with teenagers the potential damage is even bigger than with adults."

She stopped and looked at me earnestly.

Our conversation had taken an unexpected turn. It was not pleasant for either of us, but I needed to understand fully the motivational structure of this lady, in order to have a complete picture of her qualifications.

I pressed on:

> "What could this contradiction mean for you in detail; I mean in your business life?"

She immediately understood why I had asked that question – or rather, why I had had to do so. In that second both of us intuitively knew her answer would result in her taking a big career step, or destroying it.

She took her time in answering.

> "In a way I am forced to live in a state of commercial schizophrenia," she said openly and with a sad undertone, but with great honesty for which I still respect her today.
>
> "I actually live a lie. That is why a part of me wants to stop right here. My problem, though, is that I'm a single parent, that I am very well paid – and doing this work is what I am best at."

She paused.

> "I had hoped when we started talking today that this new career step would somehow relieve me of that schizophrenia, by delegating it down, away, to brand management. I just realized, as we speak, that this is not possible. I would betray myself, and would continue doing it, only on a higher income-level." This she said in a quiet voice.

We looked at each other, and I thanked her most sincerely, with great respect for what had just happened.

It goes without saying that I had to recommend to my client the other candidate. A few months later I heard that the lady had left the soft drinks business altogether. I don't know what became of her, but I hope she reads this book and realizes the high esteem in which I hold her, as the story does not completely end here.

For once I had told my own kids about that encounter, more for didactic reasons than any other, and had thought that they would swiftly forget this little story. However, years later I had a totally fascinating and most profound three-hour conversation about honesty and ethics with my then 18-year-old son, who was about to go to business school. This conversation meant a lot to both of us. For that destiny-influencing father-son conversation had been prompted by his referring to that "courageous diet drink lady".

At the time I had also shared that encounter with my colleagues in management. It had a subtle but lasting influence on our own business development strategies. In essence we became more thoughtful and more critical about the impact of our client's business on other people, and whether we truly wanted to take on projects from certain industries.

One small but concrete outcome was that for me personally, as a father of teenage kids, it became morally unacceptable to continue supporting the cigarette industry in directing its marketing push more "efficiently" towards teenagers, while at the same time I had forbidden my own kids from smoking. It was a difficult business decision to take, but I stopped working for the cigarette industry altogether.

Sometimes all it takes is the courage of one single person to speak with complete honesty. This can create an impact that moves out in ever-increasing circles, possibly helping others to find a way back to their own integrity.

# 6

# Inhuman business

We often say that the business world has become so tough over the years, that it's actually inhuman in many respects. But if something is inhuman or non-human, then what is it, really, at its core level? Who profits from it?

**Taking everything into consideration, it is more than doubtful that *we* profit from "modern business". We accept it, tolerate it, live with it, and, yes, we endure it. But do we ever really feel any love for it?**

**Again, who was it who created this business world? Regrettably *we* created it, but based on what kind of philosophy? Maybe it's time to change drastically that philosophy?**

By now it should be clear to everyone that we must look critically at our own business philosophies and how they influenced us in creating a pretty unhealthy system. Which human being in his right mind would want to live and work his whole life in an inhuman environment?

These are deep questions, and certainly not just a word game.

**It's not difficult to find examples of inhuman behaviour in business. They are more or less everywhere, even in our own firms. Yet we have a tendency to look away, normally far away. Inhuman events in business of course happen in the Third World, but in *our* country?**

Let us take a look at some hard business facts from Europe today.

I spent a lot of time researching this chapter and found many of the facts I discovered disturbing. On the other hand I want to keep this chapter short. Let me therefore single out a specific and recent incident that speaks in remarkably clear language.

**Consider this headline article in the *International Herald Tribune* in October 2009: "On October 5th 2009, Louis-Pierre Wenes, the Deputy CEO of France Telecom resigned in the wake of a spate of suicides at the company that were directly blamed on a bullying management style, abusive corporate practices and a brutal approach to restructuring."**

Well, this certainly corroborates with the "business is war" philosophy which we all have come to accept as normal. What struck me was that this took place in a modern, technology-driven, semi state-owned firm, in one of the most advanced economies of Europe.

I wanted to know more. Here is a summary. Further details are available through the Internet.

France Telecom, 52-billion Euro revenue corporate giant, employs close to 100,000 people in France and many more abroad. The company's charter states that "the French government holds a key stake in the company in order to guarantee appropriate levels of social responsibility are taken seriously by the management".

As a result France Telecom claims to have one of the highest social standards in France; its mission statement confirms the importance of and respect for its human assets, i.e. its people.

The story continued a couple of days later through various reports, a summary of which follows.

October 9th 2009: Over the past 18 months, 25 executives and staff (that number had stood at 22 when I started putting this book together in August of 2009) had killed themselves either in their offices at France Telecom or outside, as a direct result of intolerable pressure at work. In that same period at least 12 more unsuccessful business-related suicide attempts by executives or employees at France Telecom were discovered.

This all happened in a company that is highly regulated and, on paper at least, has one of the most social, employee-friendly charters in Europe.

**At the end of October 2009, I read an interesting article in the *International Herald Tribune* about this topic. In sober words it reported that the current, official suicide rate in businesses in France was 24 per 100,000 employees *per year*!**

That was quite a shock to me.

**The article gave an overview of business-related suicide rates around the world and how they had grown over the last couple of years. It continued by reporting business related suicide rates were still higher in Japan and a few other Eastern European countries, and that while the rate had substantially increased over the last couple of years, it was still considered *normal.***

At that point I became really angry.

**"*Normal?*" I asked myself. How cynical can one become? Can we be any more contemptuous of our own dignity?**

**Twenty-five years ago suicide figures or statements like these would have provoked an open outcry. If an economic system considers it *normal* that 24 people per 100,000 employees kill themselves every year, and even more attempt but fail to kill themselves because of unbearable pressures at work, then maybe something is seriously wrong with that system.**

I promised to keep this chapter short, so here are just four more titbits, details of which you can find on the Internet.

It is in the City of London, the UK's financial nerve-centre, rather than in the poor and desperate suburbs of some major UK cities, that the number of official drug-addicts has exploded since 2008. This came to the surface following the drastic reduction in bonuses which meant bankers could no longer afford to pay for their drugs, mostly cocaine. Thank heavens 2009 bonuses went up again!

Government reports from Belgium estimated that prior to the crisis in 2008 one in six middle or senior-level executives was close to burn-out or was already burnt out. Since then that ratio has deteriorated further - in 2009 it was estimated to be one in four. A burnt-out executive isn't just as useless as a burnt-out light bulb – please excuse the metaphor. He or she provides a very sad, demoralising and truly awful personal example to everyone around them.

In Austria it has been reported that every third employee will need psychotherapeutic help to cope with mounting pressures at work. Loss of meaning, intolerable business and performance pressures as well as the fear of sliding into poverty are quoted in a recent government report as prime causes for this.

The report also mentioned another tragic development: increased family violence. And don't think this phenomenon is limited to blue-collar workers. In fact it's quite the opposite, for the worst hit are white-collar families.

And to top it off, there is a large industrialized country in Europe in which over half a million children live in poverty. Poverty is defined as the inability to nourish the children with at least two warm meals per day, to provide adequate schooling and a roof over their heads. Guess which country it is? Germany! And the figures are from mid-2009.

I personally work in professional services, an industry where at least now, in the middle of 2010, we may feel slightly more immune from the growing in-humanity of modern business. But the fact that business may be even more brutal in a classical industrial, say, manufacturing, environment does not mean we should not examine our own environment carefully, critically and realistically.

What can we do?

**It would be smart and honourable to use the current situation as an incentive to help ourselves and others by using every opportunity to *ease* pressures, especially if you are in a senior management position and you have the power and position to rebuild trust and create a more dignified workplace.**

Some of us are doing that already, and, indeed, this is most honourable and necessary. But the fact is, the number of executives who are experienced and smart enough to realize that easing pressure (both on themselves and others) will help raise morale and increase efficiency, is still small.

What makes me even more concerned is that I can directly see how most top-level executives nowadays are driven by the same fears – perhaps even greater ones – as the employees they manage. But instead of managing or transforming those fears, which would constitute good and intelligent leadership in my personal opinion, they do the opposite. The opposite is inefficient leadership by forcing those fears down into the organization, where those fears then have devastating effects on motivation, communication and productivity. This is often done unconsciously, but the negative effects can be felt nevertheless.

We were not born to be natural saviours. Maybe we should be, but just preserving the dignity and quality of our own lives is already a pretty noble task, and keeps us well occupied. As a result I am not advocating that we all become saints, but I do want to encourage every reader to be fully aware of what can happen and, in fact, what *is* happening in modern business.

Let me finish this chapter by saying that we simply need to be totally alert.

# 7

# A businessman's consciousness

You didn't have to read this book to recognize that we live in challenging times. As I said at the beginning, many of us in business are deeply concerned, some of us are quite frustrated or already in pain, a few of our friends and colleagues might even be cracking.

What hurts is not only the frustration or the business pressures; the real problem lies much deeper, and is more dangerous. The real issue is the loss of meaning. But this will be the subject of another book.

**There are always several ways to deal with a problem. The smartest way is to take advantage of the problem and to *use* it intelligently! It's the same with anger. You can use anger destructively to smash something into a thousand pieces or you can use its energy constructively to propel you towards a solution, like walking out of a deeply frustrating situation.**

When analysing thousands of individual business careers – which translates into thousands of individual fates –

I saw how all ultimate roots for both challenges and solutions lie in the human consciousness. The answers and solutions to all problems lie indeed within us.

We are much better equipped to deal with problems in our business world than we think, but we need to understand all the tools at our disposal. From this we can derive actionable solutions.

Starting in greater detail in the next chapter, we will analyse and discuss seven concrete solutions.

Before we can do that, however, we should start with a quick look at our own consciousness. In my view, the consciousness of every business executive, in of fact every human being, consists of three levels. These three levels invariably make up what we call "our personality":

- **Normal Consciousness:** our standard operating procedure. It drives what we generally think and how we construct "our world".
- **The Sub-Conscious:** this drives our emotions, most of which are buried in the unconscious part of our psyche.
- **Supra-Consciousness:** the higher place of intuition and wisdom, often viewed as the level of our soul.

The terms used here are partly science-based, partly experience-based.

## Normal Consciousness level

Normal Consciousness is what we tactically use to run our "standard operations": it's mainly our mind.

Although this one key aspect of our psyche, which influences our whole life, would merit a more extensive and profound look and a detailed analysis in itself, suffice it to say here that the mind's job is essentially to create our reality.

The way it does this is by repetition. The more some views are repeated the more solid our "reality" becomes in our mind. That is also the reason why the mind does not like too much change or too many new things to integrate; it's why it dislikes contradictions and paradoxes, but loves cosy comfort zones. For the mind the world is, and will always be, in a way, unfathomable. Knowing this, the mind doesn't want you to question its wisdom, as it knows its wisdom is limited.

As a result, the mind is always stressed, always busy, cannot stop thinking, and even when we sleep it never stops its chatter.

**The mind is a fairly emotional-neutral system for analyzing everything and putting it all into boxes with names. It uses its own past experiences, mainly what it learned intellectually, as well as *our society's system of values* as a yardstick to describe the world to us: this is rational, this is how one has to behave, this is how a corporate organization works, and this is how one makes a career and so on.**

**Please note that the mind is just a *tool* used by our personality to navigate us through existence, nothing more, although if you look around, for specific reasons that we shall discuss, our society glorifies the mind and the intellect, giving them an almost "god-like" status.**

The mind, for instance, does not have the power to move us into action. The power comes from a different source, from emotions, as we will see in a moment.

The worst thing, though, about the mind, is the fact that it is "cold" – i.e. by and large utilitarian. Something has value if it suits a purpose. Whether or not that purpose has integrity, is noble or corrupt, is secondary for the mind, the intellect. If it were not the case, by the way, no person could ever betray another. But since the mind is so versatile it can find justification for more or less everything, as long as it is "useful".

The mind can create hundreds of reasons, mostly political, but equally business-driven reasons, why hurting someone is useful and therefore ultimately "good". That is the reason why dictators, power-driven politicians and other leaders are always able to find "rational" grounds for acting without integrity, manipulating and hurting people or even for starting a war. The same principle applied to the madness of the Crusades in the Dark Middle Ages and it applies equally in modern times to the wars in Iraq, Afghanistan or Africa.

Because the intellect is structured in this specific way, it is easily manipulated. It therefore does not come as a big surprise that the mind is heavily overrated by politics and our education system.

**In business it's not so different either. We are trained at business school to take "rational" decisions, when in the world of real business more or less *all* decisions are based on emotions. *Emotions* provide the energy to move us forward.**

The intellect can, and of course should be, used to prepare decisions, but in practice only 10-15 per cent of all important decisions in a human being's life are truly based on pure reason and rational analysis.

An exception would be technical optimisation models, but most readers know how small a part they play in senior or strategic management decisions.

And the rest?

Well, all other business decisions are close to 100 per cent based on emotion (of course supported by facts and some analysis).

These emotions can be positive or negative, but they are always the ultimate reason.

You smile, because you disagree? The world is rationally managed, I'm a thoroughly rational person, I hear you say.

**I can understand this only too well. Maybe you could take a moment to answer the following three questions for yourself, and *then* look again:**

**Have you ever argued with and even insisted to your boss that you yourself should *not* be promoted, but that he should award your dream-job to someone else, because your rational analysis came to the logical conclusion that this other person was truly better qualified?**

Can you swear that feelings of sympathy or antipathy have never ever influenced your decision to promote someone from your team, but that you exclusively used analytical, purely rational measurements?

Based on which purely rational parameters did you choose your car, your house, your wife or husband, or your last holiday destination?

**Our whole business system seems to work upside-down. It is made to appear purely rational when, in fact, it is not. Business decisions are *always* driven by emotions, yet hardly anyone admits it, and that is one of the key reasons why business is often so dishonest and why it creates so much stress.**

**If you have observed top-management decision-making processes for decades, as I did and still do every day, you can clearly see the interrelation between emotions and business decisions. More than that, emotionally-based strategic decisions are sometimes even rationalised *backwards*. I'm certain in your companies you have seen that happen more than once.**

In a way this is all quite funny to watch since our whole system praises rational decision-making as the ultimate truth and final solution to all problems, be it in business, science or society – when reality looks so different.

## The Sub-Conscious level

The next reason why the business world is so often an unhappy place is the following: in business you meet many people who live and work together without really being aware of what they are doing or thinking – or why they are feeling in a particular way and what they are feeling.

**What is lacking is *consciousness*.**

**People who are not trained to be conscious then have no choice but to operate out of their *sub-conscious***

**– which is the place in our being that stores all recognized *and* unrecognized emotions, as well as all *unprocessed* emotions. Consciousness operates like a strong head-light. If it is not turned on, one literally has to work and live without a clear light. In an environment like our modern business world, which is not always so transparent and has its number of dark and obscure twists and turns, this is a serious handicap. That light helps us to differentiate much better. Therefore, and not only symbolically, many business people are in the dark, especially about themselves, their subconscious motives and their own psychological structure and makeup.**

This has nothing at all to do with intelligence. People tend to confuse this. You can be highly intelligent in a logical-mechanical sense, yet be tormented by fear-based emotions, aggression or painful mental pictures coming from the subconscious, leading to irrational behaviour and decisions, for the simple reason that you are not used to shining the light of consciousness on those darker spots within your own psyche.

While only this step can give us much needed clarity, we tend to take it only when something in our life really starts to hurt.

One of the key reasons for this is that our current society is actively preventing us from taking this important step in self-awareness. Why? Because it is precisely in these deeper areas that the ego reigns. The ego is easily manipulated, whereas people who are self-aware are much harder to influence. And almost all business decisions are influenced by an ego stimulus: career struggles or even simple purchasing decisions, say, by retail customers. Just look at perfume commercials.

Let us take a look at the impact on business.

Emotions are the key provider of energy, the fuel so to speak, of all actions we take in life. It is not the intellect, the mind, whose task is more analytical. The sub-conscious is filled with emotions – and drives the ego. Problems arise because of the fact that our sub-conscious is generally a rather murky place, often filled with murky emotions. But in real business many decisions are taken from exactly this place.

What therefore counts in an ethical sense in business is the quality of our emotions. These qualities – or the lack thereof – need to be understood and addressed if we want to change something for the better in our business life. You will now also understand why, for instance, change programs in corporate culture hardly ever work out. They deal with symptoms, not with root causes.

In order not to be too abstract, here are some examples of the negative, but ever present, emotions that play a key role in driving business and management decisions on all corporate levels. (I'm certain, if you're honest, you'll recognise quite a few.)

Stark ambition, all kinds of pressure, anger, need for recognition and/or superiority, fear of competition, aggression, mistrust, jealousy, vanity, selfishness, the occasional quantum of greed, drive for power and so on.

**Please also observe that these emotions are usually strong and loud! They do not even include the *unrecognized* and *suppressed* emotions that, as any psychologist will confirm, are equally buried in the deeper levels of the psyche. These little devils also**

**have the tendency to express themselves, most of the time vengefully: hatred, shame, despair, mediocrity complexes, obsession, destructiveness, big egos and so on.**

**And now, in contrast, please be honest and consider how many key business or management decisions are taken from *this* batch of emotions, the constructive ones: joy, kindness, fairness, warmth, honesty, respect for others, compassion, the desire to create peace and quiet efficiencies, non-aggressive communication, and so on.**

Both lists are of course much longer, this is just a small selection. The reservoir of emotions in our psyche is substantial. It is the quality of our consciousness that determines which ones we utilize to energize our decisions and actions in business. By using constructive and positive emotions we manifest positive outcomes. And, most regrettably, dear reader, they also work vice versa.

Logical proof required? Having understood the above everyone can easily recognize which emotions we tend to work with, by simply looking at our world of modern business.

Again, it is the emotional quality or 'shade' of our emotions (to use a metaphor) which colours what we create. For example, if we have an action-plan (in our mind) and use the emotional quality of fear or aggression to make it manifest (a process that runs, alas, 90 per cent of the time unconsciously), then that emotional energy will remain embedded in what we have created, and it determines the fields of resonance (i.e. what we get back).

When we do something with a vengeance, knowingly destructive or dishonest, it tends to come back and haunt us. I am quite sure that every reader has experienced this, and not just once or twice, in his or her business life.

Before we return to the question of what this all means and how we can use these realizations as an antidote to an already poisoned environment, something to help bring a little light and meaning back into our business lives, we need to look at the third level of operating consciousness in our personality.

## Supra-Consciousness level

This is the place of intuition and inspiration. At this level we are in contact with the level of our soul.

**Intuition is always something personal, totally individual and feelings-based, because its task is to make certain *your* life is a success. That is why in our "rational" world, where the intellect only accepts things it can weigh or count, intuition is either ignored or often "rationalized" away.**

We therefore need, first of all, to recognize that we all have intuition, and that intuition is probably the greatest gift life has provided us with. Secondly, we need to understand its function and, thirdly, we have to train ourselves to listen to this source of information.

**Ultimately intuition (sometimes called gut feeling, although that doesn't do it full justice) is the best source of business information. After observing its workings in hundreds of business cases, I can say**

**with certainty that intuition has an overview of what is good for us now *and* in the future. It is an incorruptible guardian of righteousness and integrity. When we go against our intuition, we invariably punish ourselves by developing a "bad conscience".**

What our intuition wants for us is real success, and the sincere joy that comes with that, constructive and humanly valuable solutions,-warm, heartfelt qualities that make us feel good – and the comfort to know we have taken wise and ultimately meaningful decisions.

**Intuition, however, is always *soft*; it tends to work through subtle inner promptings, intuitive pictures in our minds and gentle feelings.**

**By contrast, our management world is very *loud*. Big and often forceful egos seem to dominate. Strong emotions, the constant undertone of fighting and aggression as well as a largely cold and primarily utilitarian approach to all business decisions, produce so much outer and inner noise, that the soft inner voices, the ones that really care for our best interests, are hard to hear.**

Here are two classic examples.

How many of you, in the middle of intense thinking about a business problem, have felt a subtle need, coming from somewhere deep inside, to just get up from your desk, take a short walk in the sun, sit on a bench for a while and quietly reflect on the issue occupying you mind?

Almost all of you, I would guess.

How many of you in reality ever followed that gentle impulse?

Well, there you go.

What did that inner voice want for you or from you? It wanted your best, your inspiration, your overview. It wanted commercial or organizational success for you. It wanted to inspire you to find your business solution without distraction, in a pure kind of way. It wanted to reduce your stress-level. It wanted to make the decision-making process more comfortable for you.

And what do we do with that gentle inner voice? We, of course, ignore it.

Here's another example: how often does that gentle inner voice send us a message, especially during tough and agitated business discussions, to soften up, to "let go", to swallow our ego and not to be so deadly serious?

It tends to speak to us at exactly those moments when the dark and unprocessed emotions from the sub-conscious that we looked at previously, boil up, take over and prevent us from following that intelligent and friendly, but always soft, inner voice.

Again, what did this intuitive inner voice want for us? It wanted us to stop wasting our emotional energy in struggling for power. It wanted to prevent emotional injuries that we inflict upon ourselves and others in those critical moments, injuries that will take a long time to heal, sometimes a whole lifetime. Intuition wants our lasting success, a success we cannot claim as ours if we hurt too many people on the way.

Personally I have always found the topic of intuitive knowledge most intriguing. For many years I have observed its workings, thought about it a lot – how it worked and why it worked – and have not shied away from discussing it with my senior colleagues. As if to provide feedback to whether we were on the right path, an opportunity arose in our own business in the mid-nineties that would test our willingness to listen to our intuition.

Here's what had happened.

Out of the blue I had been contacted by the Chairman of the Supervisory Board of a large private equity firm that had taken a major stake in a recently privatized Hungarian industrial company. In our first personal meeting the Chairman, a British gentleman, not only stressed the highly sensitive nature of his request but even demanded that both our head of research and myself sign a toughly worded confidentiality agreement before he would explain the business case.

We were intrigued – and interested.

Executive search cases like this one are rare, but they do happen – and thSey are usually quite well paid. Here's the case we were confronted with.

A new CEO was being sought for that particular Hungarian company. My colleague and I looked at each other. There was nothing new or special in this business proposition, so why the immense confidentiality? Was it that our potential client wasn't used to working with executive search methodology and didn't know that confidential assignments were our daily bread?

As it turned out he knew exactly what he wanted us to do. He explained that the Supervisory Board had already identified the ideal candidate, had even taken initial soundings, which were most positive. More than that, he, as Chairman of the Supervisory Board, and the candidate were more or less in agreement on almost all details: total compensation, starting date, and most importantly, the future strategy of the firm.

Again, my colleague and I looked at each other: What could we contribute then, since all decisions had already been taken?

The Chairman of the Supervisory Board indicated that we were needed primarily for tactical reasons. A major Hungarian firm with close government ties was still a minority shareholder and the candidate was a well-known top executive in Hungary with important political affiliations. Getting him to leave his current CEO post and joining our potential client's firm as new CEO could be reported negatively in the national press.

As a result the whole process had to be strictly formalized, executed by a reputable and well-known international executive search firm which had to make sure everything looked proper and professional.

We would be asked to present three top-level candidates, initially only on paper, but of course it was clear from the outset who would be offered the job. Possibly we might even be asked to conduct formal hearings, again, simply to look above board.

Now we understood where the need for confidentiality came from. Our reaction was a bit hesitant. The

Chairman noticed it and added that the search fee would be generous. He indicated a figure of close to US$40,000 for this executive search, which was a lot of money then, especially since we would not be expected to do a lot of work.

Easy money – and it would create a solid reputation in Hungary for our firm. The candidate was a prominent figure and the firm of our client was well known.

From our point of view, there was no problem.

Yet somehow both of us felt a hesitation in saying yes – and we did not know where that came from. We asked for two days to consider his proposal; the Chairman gave us less than 24 hours. We had to come back with a firm decision by lunchtime the next day. Obviously the matter was urgent.

After our guest had left, my colleague and I spent the rest of the afternoon analyzing and evaluating this business opportunity. Clearly we wanted to increase our business profile in Hungary, and clearly, this was the right positioning in the market-place – and it was a most profitable proposition.

**The only problem was that it didn't *feel* right.**

All intellectual, logical arguments were pro, only our intuitive feeling was contra. As we were still uncertain after hours of pondering, we called our lawyer for advice and asked if he thought we would be violating the ethical principles of our business or could somehow get into trouble by accepting this proposition. He promised he would look into it and give us feedback.

He called around 11.00 the next morning. Legally and ethically the deal was perfectly acceptable. My colleague and I wanted to go ahead, but something still held us back. We each decided to spend 10 minutes completely alone, in order to find final clarity and then to take a joint decision. When we reconvened we didn't have to say a single word: we both intuitively had decided to decline the opportunity.

After I had called the Chairman of the Supervisory Board I felt strange; actually I felt really bad. The Chairman had reacted very angrily on the phone and sworn never to consider using our services again.

Out of interest we followed the subsequent events: three candidates were presented by one of our competitors; the "right" candidate, of course, won. He got good press and our competitor did too. At that moment we realized that we had completely screwed up. It would have been so easy.

Over the following months we forgot the matter until – about a year later – the Chairman of the Supervisory Board was ousted and the new CEO was also ousted and sued.

They were accused of cooperating to embezzle millions of dollars in a large take-over transaction. Because of the large Hungarian minority shareholder, as far as I can recall, the case led to a parliamentary hearing, in the course of which our competitor had to testify.

Of course, it came out that the selection process had been rigged. Our competitor had to pay back the search fee to his client firm, and was ordered to pay a substantial penalty on top. Their reputation was in a shambles.

We were speechless – and in many ways, also deeply grateful. It could have been us.

It was not so much the fact that money had been embezzled, for, after all these were the wild days of Eastern Europe. What hit our research director and myself was the curious fact that some authority in our own consciousness had clearly been able to see into the future – and had warned us both through an intuitive feeling!

# 8

# Seven effective antidotes

Understanding the three levels of consciousness, recognizing how they operate in the business world and then using them wisely is mission-critical in our efforts to review, reassess or reconstruct our business lives.

The whole business system, however, is biased against us through pressure, constant inner and outer noise and social norms that ridicule people who seriously want to look after their own lives.

**I suppose this is the prime reason why so often senior executives feel their personal lives have been emptied, even poisoned, by *demanded* behaviours and *demanded* actions that are on a human level non-valuable and not in alignment with their true selves.**

As a result instead of providing us with energy, this kind of business and management behaviour increasingly drains our life force; it empties us out. The empty space is then often filled with self-doubt, of course never openly expressed, and if we continue, often with illness.

Dear reader, if any of the above has struck a chord within you, you may be in a bit of trouble, but, then again, you may now be ready for action.

Unfortunately the system is not only poisonous, it is also very contagious. What we therefore need is a set of effective antidotes.

Here are seven antidotes to thwart the Devil's plan. Each one is a solution in itself; applied together they are truly powerful. Once intelligently applied, these antidotes help restore meaning and re-create a higher level of personal fulfilment, and yes, even happiness, in management and business.

Let's start with a time-tested, simple, but guaranteed-to-work antidote.

## Antidote No. 1: Shine your light

This may not sound like much, but, boy it flies!

Nothing beats the light of a clear and focused consciousness, whether in business, in society at large, or in any of our personal relations. It is the strongest of all antidotes at our disposal.

**In modern society we are not trained to act consciously; we are even actively discouraged to use the full repertoire of consciousness tools available. The danger in all of this is serious, especially in business. If we do not train ourselves to turn on the light of consciousness, which as a process is simple but then again not easily done, there's a real danger that we end up wasting our unique, precious and singular life-energy – which we should remember is *limited* for every human being!**

We waste our own life-energy by acting out questionable values and sometimes destructive emotions, which inflict damage on ourselves and others in the process, especially in business and management situations.

We are all free to take decisions. Every time we take business decisions, be they related to people, strategy, operations or processes, we should decide to take decisions that are "light", rather than "dark".

Be conscious!

You have the gifts of intelligence, of differentiation and of intuition, so use them.

**Our original and natural knowledge of how the human psyche works has been clouded, even manipulated, by society's rules. Remembering how reality is created through the three levels of consciousness is *the* key to starting a change process.**

Try it!

You will soon see that even taking small decisions, so long as they reflect constructive emotions like joy, kindness, fairness, sincerity, honesty, respect for others, and most important, love for your own life, will make you feel damned good. And in the end isn't that exactly what we all want to feel? And the more of it, the better.

## Antidote No. 2: Don't feed the system with more negative energy

**Remember, the Devil needs negative emotional energy, and lots of it. In fact, this is his *food*!**

Only human beings can provide it. Without it, he would starve. In order to make sure we keep him alive and well-fed, the Devil created – through us – a business system that throws off enormous supplies of negative energy.

Unless, of course, we stop buying into his rules of the game!

Although the more mature senior executives do everything in their personal power to create an environment of trust in their firms, in reality, our whole business and commercial system is based on distrust. We very often pretend and proclaim the opposite, but it is simply not true.

**Distrust is one of the prime, indeed the worst, source of negative energy in business. And it is *everywhere*!**

Want a little proof? If we truly trusted each other – our management, our shareholders, our suppliers, all our colleagues, our staff or even our clients – we would not need so many contracts, plans, budgets, assurances, armies of controllers, battalions of lawyers, and so forth. We would not have to build in so many covenants and always have to be so defensive, would we?

The sad truth is: we don't trust others because we don't trust life.

But it gets worse: we don't trust ourselves either, and in the final analysis, we don't trust God. No wonder, as all our organized religions teach us to fear God.

But whom do we trust?

We trust society's information although we have long seen and understood at a very deep personal level that this source of information is unreliable, misleading, manipulative and damaging to our lives.

We trust a source of information that tells us life is essentially dangerous, always unfair and a constant fight.

We tend to believe it uncritically and our mind obligingly constructs reality this way for us, reconfirming our view.

We trust a source that says: Always be on the lookout and be willing to hit the other one first. There is no kindness, there is only competition. Business is war.

**We trust a system that for purely selfish reasons tries to destroy trust between human beings. All society, all media, politics especially and even the religions argue in favour of this system, because it's good for *their* business.**

Think about that for a moment.

It's time to wake up and learn. Read the story of Cain and Abel, and you realize whom we have been listening to and influenced by the most. Remember, lending his ear to that source didn't do Cain much good, and it won't do you, dear reader, any good either.

So let us be firm in cutting the system off from this negative energy and information source. It is high time to trust ourselves, to trust our own knowledge of what is truly good for us. It is high time to trust our intuitive feelings!

The first ones to benefit, by the way, are us ourselves. Why? Because it is costing us such a large amount of our daily life-energy to work and to survive in, or to even manage, this energy-draining system.

Before we start a short but interesting mental experiment together, here's a little story from my own executive life. It may not be a great story, and it took place in a smaller organization, where everything is easier, but the important thing I guess is that it took place at all.

At some stage in my early forties I realized just how much energy it was costing me personally to deal with the often frustrating business environment: the corporate politics, the little manipulations of numbers for our budgets, the gossip, the constant need for positioning, the small manipulative half-truths sowed here and there, and ultimately, the subtle undertone of distrust.

Dealing with it cost me a lot of time and effort – and a lot of nerves – and at some stage I was really sick and tired of it. I was lucky in a way as, being CEO of the firm, I had the power to work on these culture issues.

But how do you build trust in an environment that promotes distrust as a standard operating procedure? You cannot demand or ordain it top-down.

It had to start with my own behaviour. Remembering the words of a great sage, "Do not fight the darkness, but transform the darkness through the light", I decided to try a way which would surprise and hopefully challenge our people. Moreover, if it backfired, it would not cause too much harm to business operations.

In one of the senior staff meetings, I focused the discussion on the values of openness, trust and transparency – everyone agreed and nodded their full approval.

Of course, I hadn't expected anything else.

Then I took time reminding everyone of the direct commercial relationship between value-creation and trust in a corporate organization – and how it works the reverse way too.

Warming to my talk I finally said that I wanted to create a more trusting environment and that I trusted the integrity of each one of my colleagues. As a result, despite the fact that occasionally I had to deal with confidential business and personnel issues, from now on in my office I would not keep any cupboard locked, as I had nothing to hide.

It wasn't a big thing, of course, only small proof to the organization that I was serious. It goes without saying that it took everyone slightly by surprise, but that had been my goal.

I continued by saying that wasting time and energy through politics was not acceptable any more. Not only for atmospheric reasons alone but for basic commercial reasons as well. That is why I had taken the above step.

It took us all a while to adapt to a more open and trustworthy environment. The rewards, however, were felt by everyone.

Step by step our culture changed and helped to avoid silly emotional conflicts. It also educated everyone to deal with their – real or imaginary – conflicts through themselves first. Last but not least it also forced me to be truthful and to think more carefully before I took or communicated a management or people-related decision.

Now here's a little confession: for about one month I had marked all folders containing confidential financial or personnel information so I could see the next morning, if anyone had stuck their nose in them.

The trust in my colleagues was well rewarded: it was great to see that no one ever did!

Let us now do a short mental experiment to expand on the above.

Imagine that in one of the ten largest industrial nations in the world – overnight – an army of business angels appears and convinces every executive board in that country to change course completely and make trust and transparency their one and only, in fact their absolute and immediate, priority – and that all senior executives wake up the next morning and act upon this.

What do you think would happen?

Now, the trick and indeed the benefit for you here, dear reader, is not to do an intellectual analysis, but to watch your first emotional response.

What is the first emotional reaction?

**Don't be disappointed if your reaction is either fully negative or at least split between positive and negative (you *feel* that it would be too good to be true, yet *think* at the same time this could never work).**

**Your reaction shows you two key aspects about *yourself.***

Firstly, how much you hold as an ingrained belief that distrust is indeed the real basis for the system; and, secondly, it shows you your subconscious fears, that you could personally fail in such an honesty-driven and trust-based system. (And that is why subconsciously you reject it.)

Interesting, isn't it?

**So what is it about an integrity, trust and honesty-based system? We all seem to want it; we proclaim it daily, especially with clients; we fervently demand it from others; and we even make it part of our mission statements in business. Yet we don't live it, and in reality, we often don't even *want* it.**

Ah, the Devil's manipulative power.

Not to worry. I have done this experiment many times: 9 out of 10 executives react negatively – at first.

Let's use our tool, our mind, to think and then to reconstruct our reality. Following on from the above example, and taking the UK as an example, how long would it take for the whole country to move to the new system?

**My personal guess would be four or five years, because I have seen that once a system turns, it gains momentum, unexpectedly quickly. Everyone, after conquering their initial fears, at some stage starts to feel the soothing emotional benefits of a *really* integrity-based economic system. As a next step everyone wants**

**to be in with the good guys, and you recognize them quickly.**

Imagine then the following situation: the country's business leaders decide to call major conferences on one particular day, nationwide, within their firms, inviting as many participants as logistically possible (all the workforce, management, suppliers, shareholders and so on).

Then they make public statements such as the following: "Our revenue and earnings per share estimates for the coming reporting season were too aggressive. We already knew that but nevertheless worked with these figures, essentially out of fear and pressure from our boards. We apologise to everyone, including our shareholders, for not having been honest with them and ourselves. We promise that this will change as of today.

"We also realized that we could only achieve such aggressive targets, if we squeezed everyone to the maximum, especially our people who are truly our most valued resource, but equally our suppliers, who would then do the same to us and to their sub-suppliers.

"To our clients nationally and worldwide we say this: Our products and services will from now on reflect only high qualities, for which we stand by personally, with our new-found integrity."

These would certainly be strong, authentic and emotionally powerful messages. So different from the often empty and meaningless corporate statements we usually hear.

At first, it's probably fair to guess that nobody in the rest of the business world would believe it. Most international competitors would call it a cheap marketing trick, primarily because they would be fearful of the results.

But step-by-step investors would rather start buying shares of companies with real transparency and at least a good chance of true integrity (compared to the current system). Likewise consumers would increasingly buy products and services of companies where, step-by-step, they could rely on what was promised.

Furthermore, once the workforce sees that top management is serious, the need for manoeuvring and political in-fighting, say, between trade unions and management, would slowly recede.

Employees would start to see that their work was more appreciated; also, under the new management system, they would get honest and compassionate feedback if it was not good. Increasingly the system would honour honesty, including the freedom of career choice. Some people would leave their jobs and would find it natural to start doing something that made more sense to their talents, but they would not feel ashamed of it and the system would accept it. The rest who stay in business would find it much more rewarding and would be more motivated.

Undue sick leave, mobbing, destructive and mostly unnecessary internal emotional conflicts, and manipulation of various sorts would slowly end.

Secondary effects would follow: for example, manipulation of research results, a major problem in every industry that produces for the mass consumer markets, would slowly stop.

Fairly quickly, product quality everywhere would go up. Fewer products with negative side-effects would come to the market, as these side-effects would become known.

Dishonest civil servants would be ousted, incapable politicians as well; bribery and manipulative scientific research would come to an end. Financial manipulation would become more difficult, aggressive and greedy behaviour less accepted in society.

Profit levels would initially fall but would then recover as the system moves towards greater balance. Marketing would swiftly become a source of valuable information based on truth and integrity, and would be less used as an aggressive and manipulative tool to push products. This would reduce marketing expenses and with it cost of sales. Consumer trust would be won over.

The list goes on and on.

Will the above miraculous transformation ever happen?

Probably not.

But then, who knows what the business world will look like in 30 years. I have the strong impression that younger executives and indeed many MBA students throughout Europe, a region where I can observe what happens, have lost their uncritical faith in the system and are actively challenging its values. For the first time in decades of observation I can see that they are following different values; I sense a considerably stronger willingness to help each other and to cooperate instead of accepting a system-enforced, almost religious fervour to aggressively compete and fight.

We have the chance, maybe the responsibility, to support that next generation by creating a business environment that is more truthful and acts more consciously.

So, let's consciously be aware of those occasions when we create, or allow others to create, negative emotional energy – and then take action to stop it.

## Antidote No. 3: Detox

You may well think what detoxing has to do with cutting off the Devil's energy from our lives.

In fact, it has a lot to do with it. We live in a terribly polluted and truly poisonous environment, more or less 24/7.

The water in every large European city is almost as polluted as the air. Most of the food we eat is contaminated and/or damages our health. And I am not only referring to the cheap and industrialized food, unhealthy diets or simply too much fat that we eat, which is just a part of the overall dilemma.

**We are overweight for two other key reasons. Firstly, because our bodies can no longer get rid of the incoming pollution that we incessantly feed it quickly enough. Secondly, the body puts on weight as sheer armour to deal with the increased daily stress levels, especially the psychological stress we are under.**

Hardly anything we consume – air, water, food and a number of other things we don't associate with this intake process, such as information – is natural anymore, let alone pure. Like many of our roads, our arteries become increasingly congested, thus destroying the quality of our lives. The amount of noise pollution we regularly suffer is clearly damaging our health. The radiation from mobile telephones, computer and television screens, wireless connectivity, etc., causes massive stress to our endocrine systems.

Our psyches have become an unbalanced pandemonium of emotional and mental trash, fed daily by poisonous thoughts and negative mental images mainly through the mass media. If you have enough discipline and enough love for your own life, stop watching the news for just five days, maybe when you are on holiday. You really owe it to your intelligence to try. After five days you'll understand how your psyche is bombarded with garbage that hardly ever represents any true value.

Shall we stop, because, really, it gets a bit too painful?

If you were to visit our society from a different star you would wonder why we in the Western world all live such insane lives. Even more surprising is the fact that hardly anyone living in this "modern society" notices the insanity anymore. Even worse, living this kind of life is accepted as normal by everyone, is propagated by industry and undisputed by a conniving government that truly should know much better.

We seem to forget that every system in nature that is inundated with pollution soon gets sick. We humans are no exception. The body can of course deal with a certain amount of pollution, but these days pollution is coming from everywhere.

A pure psyche would be the best and most effective remedy, as any Zen monk can attest to, but even that part of our being has become soiled and polluted.

Do you remember how soothing it was to walk in pure, unspoilt nature, in clean and crisp air, with an uncluttered mind, joyfully filled with constructive thoughts and completely free of any stress or time pressure? Of being in an environment where the sounds you hear are natural, where you can drink water that is crystal clear and where the colours surrounding you are intense and stimulating, creating a paradise of visual beauty?

A pure psyche will feed you the yearning for such a life.

In business, how often do you meet a person who has warmth and clarity in their eyes, who radiates an honest and relaxed intelligence, completely free from any manipulative tendency, who through his gentleness and wisdom commands respect, who through thoughtful speech displays depth of character and the serenity of a truly independent thinker, whose behaviour is sincere and natural and who through his presence gives you a great gift: your reinvigorated trust in man's essential goodness?

We don't meet too many of those people in business, do we?

**Here's my advice: If you want to have such an encounter in business, detox with determination and on *all* levels, and become such a person yourself.**

## Antidote No. 4: Find your mission in life

This is more easily said than done, but it is quintessential that you do it. If you don't do it yourself, fate may do it for you. It can be with a friendly nudge or with a firm kick in the butt. So it's better to be smart and pro-active.

In order to master this one we need to come back to a pivotal question we addressed earlier: "What am I doing with my (business)-life and does what I do professionally suit my character and talents?"

Remember that we operate in a political, economic and religious system that was forcefully set up by powers that gave you – and indeed anyone – no say. These powers had only one interest at heart: their own. The fact that they constantly claim the opposite makes them even more untrustworthy.

I know it sounds harsh, but these powers have no idea who you are, they don't know what you need – and in practice they couldn't care less.

The system wants you to work your rear end off and make no trouble (business); to shut up, give away your authority and ask no questions (the political system); and to believe in an authority whose record of salvation, enlightenment or establishing lasting peace can only be described as a sad and dire failure (religion).

Yet it is exactly to these powers that we have given our lives, and I mean, completely. It is their values we live by, not our own. Not too intelligent of us, come to think of it.

I realize these are tough words, but we live in decisive times. You either try to live much more consciously, get your life in order and take really good care of it, or you don't. Nobody else will do it for you.

**With these powers *not* supporting us, we would imagine finding out who we are, what is good *for us* and what our mission in life is, is not that easy.**

Yet it is not so difficult, as we shall see. I can promise you that this journey to your true self will be exciting, sometimes very funny, always valuable, and worth every effort.

Everybody who comes here comes with an individual mission. A system of talent and inner longing will create a desire to do something that will provide meaning to your life.

**The secret here is that if you do something that is *meaningful* you will derive energy from that activity. Likewise if you indulge in activities that drain energy out of your life because they are not meaningful for you, you can be certain that you are on the wrong track.**

Think of the tremendous energy you had when you went on your first date with your first true love. Nothing could stop you, you had endless energy. Then by way of contrast, think of the energy level you had when you attended the third budget meeting this quarter, run by an aggressive and demanding boss who is under huge pressure himself.

Over the years I have talked about these very deep questions with many senior executives. A key question came up again and again: How can I be certain that what I do is meaningful for my life, given that there are always periods of struggle that cost me my life-energy, although in general my business activity provides me with a good and comfortable level of energy?

Of course there will always be short periods when you have to concentrate hard or gather all your energy in order to overcome an obstacle. But that is not what is meant here.

***Meaning* is something lasting, something which provides a deep feeling of more or less unshakeable satisfaction, a meaning that is at least medium-term in nature. For good reason life sometimes gives us small tests to see if we are determined enough in following our mission. But, as I said above, these tests and obstacles are *always* short-term.**

By the way, you can tell if these are short-term obstacles and tests, or if you are going down the wrong path in life, through your intuitive feelings for them.

If you run up against the same hurdles again and again, if you fight endless fights that frustrate you, if you ask yourself if this is the right job, the right task, the right industry for more than 12 months, then the likelihood that you're heading in the wrong direction is close to 100 per cent.

Through my work I had innumerable opportunities to look at and analyse in great detail complete lives of business executives; their individual fates, so to speak, neatly rolled out in front of me. Through thousands of extensive interviews with senior executives, I can say I have become something of an expert in seeing if someone is merely "doing a job" or if he or she is following their mission; if what they are doing is right for their character and talent, and indeed for their soul.

**I made it my mission in business to research deeply and get to know in detail that particular aspect of my candidates. Not only has that helped our business, indeed it helped me *and* my clients. I also made it my business to speak openly with executives about this question, and to be absolutely frank with them. I know from many responses, some of which came years after these often intense encounters, that by firmly focusing business executives on the three key questions, I had helped many of them. I helped them avoid pain and frustration later on.**

As a reminder of their importance, here are the three questions again:

- **Does the work I do truly suit my talents and character?**
- **Does it match my personal vision of how I want to live?**
- **Does it make me happy?**

It goes without saying that the people who follow their mission in life are invariably more successful. This is logical. If you professionally follow the right career track, the appropriate level of responsibility, the right level of seniority, then life provides you with ample energy to succeed.

**If you do what is not right for you, life drains your energy – and rightly so! Just think of the bad conscience**

**you had when you did something sincerely wrong in your firm or when you betrayed somebody's trust, in business or in your private life. Your energy level went *down*. That's the feedback you always get from your consciousness. Of course you can try to rationalize almost everything away, but that inner authority is incorruptible.**

Contrary to what society wants you to believe, life means well for you. Your intuition carefully, almost lovingly, guides you towards what is good for you – and away from what hurts you.

How often have we heard it said that, "with hindsight, this event turned out to be a true blessing in disguise?"

Think about the "blessings in disguise", what they really are and how many you may have missed already because you trusted the wrong source of information!

We are often tempted to follow the calling of our ego with its blind ambition, acting out society-based and outdated role- and value-models that are simply unsuited to us. Most of us get depressed when we fail to land that big success or when we don't get that important job or when we are relieved of our duties against our wishes. However, in almost all cases there is deeper meaning behind such events.

We need to seek to understand; we need to get the whole picture, instead of complaining about an unjust life.

Often what hurts in those moments is the ego. Our soul, however, is relaxed, because it has the overview.

Here some examples to illustrate this point.

**There is the story of the husband who after paying a huge sum of money to go on an exclusive cruise, almost killed his wife because it was her fault they had narrowly missed the cruise ship's departure. The name of the cruise ship? It was the *Titanic.***

Paulo Coelho, the world famous best-selling author described in an interview how when he was in his mid-thirties he had decided, after months of pondering, to once and for all give up his childhood dream to become an author. He described how on one particular night he simply could not imagine anymore how being a writer could ever work out, mentally arguing to himself that he would never survive financially.

That particular night Coelho finally forced himself to be "realistic", as he said, especially since he had just been offered a major promotion in his job as a recording executive for CBS Records in the US, and had to make a decision.

**In mentally preparing for the conversation he was scheduled to have with the EVP from New York the next day, he fell asleep. The next morning he was informed by telephone that not only would he *not* be getting that important job, but that he was fired. No reasons were given.**

Coelho was devastated. He described in the interview how angry and desperate he was, how totally abandoned by God he felt. It took him a while to find a good job again. Having to earn money in the meantime, in addition to his new regular job, he started to write articles and even theatre plays which won him the attention of a publisher. The rest of course is legendary, as Paulo Coelho went on to sell over 100 million copies of his books and become one of the most read authors of all time.

Then there is Joanne Rowling. Her career is similar to Paulo Coelho's. It was through being made redundant and having no job which gave her the time and impetus to write books and the amazingly successful Harry Potter series.

Of course, society might tell you otherwise, appealing to the most primitive levels of your consciousness: you must fight aggressively; pain and sacrifice is normal. Life is about suffering and you are no exception. And don't forget to sue those bastards in New York!

But if you buy into that, you will end up with an unhappy life. If you follow society's rules you are likely to miss the point. You will probably destroy the beautiful opportunities that fate wants to grant you – because fate believes you deserve them. If you follow the rules of others, instead of your own inner awareness, you will probably prevent "blessings in disguise" from occurring in your life.

Remember Joanne Rowling, Paulo Coelho and many others. Life had to help them a little for them to find their true calling.

Trust your intuition to firmly show you your mission. Work with fate, not against it. It will always win in any case.

## Antidote No. 5: Truly understanding your thoughts, emotions and feelings

We should always look carefully at why our life is presenting us with certain events – and take the time and effort to reflect on that. The art is to reflect deeply.

First we have to get rid of the outer noise; then the same for the inner noise. The outer noise is much easier to get rid of. Essentially we need a quiet place, a turned-off mobile phone and the will power to do something good for our own life.

The inner noise is trickier, because thoughts swirl around our mind all the time – and most of these prompt emotions, adding to the inner noise level. The inner noise is like a blocking door that consists of a whirl of chaotic thoughts and emotions. Once we have worked through that filter we can enter the realm of pure feeling, where the real answers usually lie.

Meditation is a possible way to achieve this state of tranquillity. In meditation one is specifically trained to "quieten the chatter of the mind". This is done for very good reasons as we have seen but it may take a while to achieve that. For me I wanted something faster. I will show you in a minute how I did this.

**It should be obvious by now that our intuitive feeling, not our intellectual mind, is one of the *prime* tools for guiding us through life. I'm always amazed how few, otherwise highly intelligent, people take the time to *analyse* this tool, and then work with it.**

To use another metaphor, it's like starting a long distance-journey in a car, without first having learnt to read a map. Why did you not learn how to do this? Because the manufacturers of navigational systems told you that there's no need for it. But at some stage all of us get stuck. No wonder there are so many mental accidents on the road of life.

**If you consciously analyse your intellectual mind, you will notice all of a sudden that it hardly ever stops**

**talking. Your intellectual mind has an opinion about *everything*, no matter whether it is being asked for an opinion or not. Its opinions are the thoughts it produces.**

Stopping the mind from producing thoughts would, to some people, be akin to death. Of course that is not true, otherwise all Zen monks would have committed suicide by now as a result of their deep meditation. In fact these beings are so alert, so focused and yet so immensely friendly – and usually very healthy – that we should all envy them.

Back to our problem.

The real problem with the mind's constant chatter is the effect it has on emotions. Not all, but the majority of our thoughts produce emotions which cause additional noise, in effect thickening the noise filter we would need to move through.

A little trick to help us symbolize thinking is to imagine a wall with a small mouse hole in it. Imagine you are sitting in front of this mouse hole and waiting for the mouse to come out. As you do so, still your mind and define the next mouse coming out as your next thought.

While focusing on the mouse hole your mind becomes completely still – and you will enjoy that peace. Beginners are able to keep this mental stillness for about two or three seconds, before they are flooded again with thoughts. Try it yourself; it's interesting to observe.

I never made it to more than 30 seconds, but it taught me a lot. I could observe the flooding of my consciousness with thoughts, most of which were irrelevant. Once I understood this I came to see the great advantage of meditation. My personal problem at the time was that meditation was a bit too slow at the beginning. I wanted something faster. As a result I decided to use another avenue: authority!

I told my mind in no uncertain terms to shut up and stop its useless chatter, immediately! The mind's reaction was amazing. I guess for the first time my mind was being given a sharp command from true authority, to which it was not used to.

Bang!

Stillness.

What a pleasure.

My mind needed at least a full minute to recover from its shock, before it tried to reassert its authority by trying to persuade me that it was, indeed, me. But the spell was broken once and forever. From that moment onwards it was clear that my mind was a helpful tool, and that it formed an important part of my being. Nowadays I can tell my mind to shut up in a friendly way. It will listen and leave me alone for a while. I can say we have become almost friends.

The benefit is considerable.

The absence of chattering thoughts allows you to work with your intuition. It also helps you to observe your feelings, as well as your emotions, much more clearly. And remember they are the driving forces in everyone's life!

***Emotions* are loud and fly about (*emovere* – to eject, in Latin): anger, jealousy, doubts, etc. While *feelings* are usually very deep: kindness, peace, trust, etc. *Emotions* are mostly hysterical; *feelings* are sincere. *Emotions* are treacherous; *feelings* are reliable. *Emotions* are often aggressive; *feelings* tend to be soft.**

Of course some of us want to have lives which are often hysterical and aggressive, thus creating a flurry of emotional intensity. If that is your personal choice, that is absolutely fine and must by all means be respected.

**In the end, what counts is to understand how emotions and feelings work in your life. Then, and only then, can you take conscious decisions. But by now hopefully you should be clear about which one of the *feelings* you can trust to lead *your life* in the right direction.**

## Antidote No. 6: Take well-prepared action

In no way am I advocating that you should change career or jump ship at the whim of a capricious emotional flare. Our bosses yell at us from time to time and there are occasions we get upset or frustrated by some event at work.

I don't have too much admiration for people who want to be architects one year, businessmen the next, and if they fail again, entertainers or pilots, or what have you, thereafter. This is often superficial.

We have to be systematic if we want clarity. We carry responsibilities and what we decide about our business life and future must have sound substance to it.

First, we need to review what our business life has taught us so far. What have we learned and understood about our talents, our character and most importantly, about our mission? Or simply put, about our personal happiness?

Make it an exercise to write down (on a special notepad devoted to this singular purpose) the three to five most important things that your business life has taught you. No more than five, because we want to remain focused.

As a next step write down your three most important weaknesses which your business life has shown you.

**Then comes one of the most important, and in many ways, most profound parts: take an honest inventory of what you have *sacrificed* for your career up to this point in time. Be ruthlessly honest to yourself. Try to be unemotional, although in practice, this is almost impossible. If it happens, let it happen. Feelings of guilt and sadness are normal during this process, and they are human.**

Once you are clear about the above, consider what you are still willing to sacrifice for your career – and then reflect deeply and decide where it has to end.

This is a very important part. Don't hold back. Again, be ruthless. You are doing this for yourself, for a better life.

You may have sacrificed many things along the way; some were worth it, others not so.

In that process please devote a section to answering this question: What opinions about yourself and about society did you have that made you sacrifice certain things or values in your life? Are these opinions still relevant – or have you changed and grown in perception and maturity? A goal, also in terms of self-development, may have been relevant when you were 30, but no longer so now. Likewise values that meant little to you at aged 35 may now be truly important.

This inventory is a kind of initial roadmap.

It is important to do it slowly. Take your time, let it rest within yourself. I have done this myself and have done it with a number of senior executives. They all confirmed that it was truly worth it.

After a couple of days we can address the next set of questions.

**Now that you have documented what you have learned about yourself, your aspirations and your limits, we need to *do* something with this information.**

Does your current position, or the one you expect to have in your next career step, allow you to make full use of your talents?

Does your job now give you a deep sense of fulfilment?

How is your energy level, in the office, on your job, in the factory – on average?

Do you still have good feelings when going to the office every day, doing the work you do? Or is getting out of bed and getting started requiring more and more effort?

Are you permanently exhausted or do the positive moments easily outweigh the moments of stress?

Does the job, on balance, provide you with positive energy – i.e. does it invigorate you and support your life at the level of well-being, or does it drain energy from you?

Does the level of stress you experience do any damage to your health, to your creativity, to your joy in life, to your personal relationships?

What is your crystal-clear priority?

What do you want?

**What do you *need*?**

I remember reading an interview with Juergen Schrempp, the former Chairman and CEO of Daimler Chrysler (as it was then called), discussing amongst other topics why he got divorced. He said that he had taken an inventory of his life and had realized that he had energy only for one of two things: his CEO job or his family. He thought that family was less important to him.

It would not have been my own choice, but that guy's clarity was impressive. He analysed – and then acted – and got divorced.

Of course making a choice such as Schrempp did is not altogether wise. A human being can love and nourish you; a technocratic function – and all senior management jobs are technocratic functions – cannot.

It seemed fate had a little technocratic feedback for Schrempp because within a year he was fired.

When you undertake the above exercise, remember to make it profound, absolutely true, even holy, as it will make your life whole, if you do it right.

Through this individual and honest analysis, you will reach one of the following three conclusions:

**1. You like your job, find it invigorating, want to give it your best and you want to stay in it.**

No more than 25 per cent of all executives I analysed came to that conclusion.

**2. You are largely *not* happy with the way you live your business-life.**

The writing on the wall is clear: continue this way and you, or something else important to you, will suffer. But you don't know how to change it. Based on my many years of observation, about 50-60 per cent of all executives fall into this category. If I'm right, and this is what the data shows, then our society and our businesses are in very dangerous waters.

**3. The remainder of you are unsure and cannot make up your mind.**

You don't want to decide or are simply too afraid to decide about such a principal question in life.

Let us look at group No.3 first, because we can learn a lot from this.

Who and what is this group so afraid of? Essentially they are afraid of three things:

- that society will ridicule them if they take their life into their own hands, or
- that they will not have the will-power or the courage to change, or
- that they will lose their financial or other forms of security.

The bad news I have for this group is that indecision hardly ever helps. Business life has its own way of bringing events to a head, and while hesitation is logical and understandable, the likelihood of some external event "helping" that group towards a decision is high. Years of observation proves it beyond doubt.

All security can be taken away in a single moment, and people who are not happy with what they do and radiate either inertia, deep frustration or weak decision-making power are often let go first. Knowing this, they often pretend and over-act, which makes matters even worse.

So, if you are in this group, good luck. Keep at it, analyse your fears and critically check if they are truly justified or not.

Look carefully at your own mind-set in order to understand where the fears come from, but continue to love your life, remember its value to you and be on the lookout for some helpful synchronicities. This, after all, is the language of life when it talks to humans.

If you belong to the first group of 25 per cent, there is a high chance that your mind, your feelings and your soul are working in unison and that following your career track is the right way to fulfil your mission in life. At a very deep level of your being, you probably know that you are perfectly well equipped to deal with the coming business challenges and that dealing with them is your way to express who you are and how you wish to grow.

Be alert and use your capacities to make the very best of it. Perform your job with increasing kindness; make it your moral responsibility to help and support your fellow executives. Increase your level of honesty with yourself and others; increase your integrity even further.

**Teach others the importance of caring. Use business as a means to dignify your life. It *is* possible and constitutes a most noble achievement.**

Make it your task to see as many fulfilled people in your daily business life as possible, as your way to of saying "Thank you". Life may have put you into this function to do just that. This way you will create a spiral of energy that may help to protect you in the coming times.

**Now let's move to the largest (second) group. These are the ones who clearly feel an urgent need to change, and who *want* to act.**

**In the corporate world there are many functions to choose from to use as an example. I have chosen sales and sales management to illustrate a way out: *Pars pro toto* this will also apply to other functions, such as finance, manufacturing, supply chain, R&D, human resources and, last but not least, general management.**

## Sales Management

If you are in sales, sales management or business development, analyse your talents and your personality. Then analyse which part of the job you most like doing and which part you least like doing. Try not to be superficial in your analyses (eg, "In sales I don't like the weekly administrative parts, like reporting figures"). Instead, you need to go much deeper.

For sales and business development: Do you truly have a sales personality, or not?

For sales management: Do you have the required motivational, organizational and leadership skills, or not?

You will know the answers intuitively, beyond any doubt. If you are still uncertain, ask someone you trust, such as your partner or a close friend. Experience shows that their answers can be very enlightening.

Are you in sales because: it was the only job open and you stuck with it? Or is it because it offered good money? Or is it because it allowed you more freedom than other corporate jobs? Or is it because through sales you can express your personality?

Or was it because of any other relevant reason?

Are you truly capable of managing people and processes? Why have you followed a career in management? Was it the money, the power, the perceived "better life"?

How much of your original goals have became reality?

List your true motives. List the true outcomes.

**The more materialistic, status or fear-induced your original motive, the higher the likelihood that this job or function will *not* provide fulfilment.**

If you want to change, then you should actively look for sales management positions where you can better express your being, where you can live your personality, or where you will have a deeper emotional relationship with the products sold. It can be within the same industry or in another one. Look, analyse, research, but don't put yourself under too much time pressure. What is important is that you take the decision in principle. For by doing so, you set synchronicities in motion that will help you. Then very often a bit of information or a person, by accident, comes your way, and helps you further along the way. Looking out for synchronicities is what the really smart guys are doing.

What have you got to lose? What is worth more: a 30k per annum higher salary with possibly even more frustration and more work, or a function that is fulfilling and pays ok? You decide.

Throughout my business life I have always decided to go for job fulfilment first and foremost. And that's the advice I have given to thousands of senior executives. Since I – and all the others who have done it – truly liked (yes enjoyed) what we were doing, we did our work pretty well. And as with everything you do well, you usually end up being recognized, promoted and making good money. (The spiral goes downwards, of course, in situations opposite to this.)

There is a rule of thumb that has worked for decades: if you are happy with what you are doing most of the time (i.e. between 80 and 85 per cent of your time) then you are probably in the right place. During the remaining 15 to 20 per cent of your time, there will be problems, but as long as they're short-term and not structural problems, that's ok. It seems that we human beings need problems to keep us alive.

A key question everyone in management should ask themselves is the following (again I take sales management as an example): How well equipped are you to deal with complexity in either sales processes or sales management functions?

**It's perfectly okay *not* to like complexity, even to reject it – for yourself. In the end it's your working days which suffer. Some corporate organizations just love to create complexity, especially in sales and business development. A lot of it is unnecessary, hyped-up, counterproductive and bullshit. (Apologies to my friends in organizational development departments. I know you meant well!).**

**Nevertheless, after observing senior sales executives for many years, it becomes so very clear, that increased complexity *never* solves a problem but *always* creates more problems: increased problems in process management, increased problems in communication, increased problems in motivating people and so on. Lots of energy gets wasted, on all levels, including the precious time of the senior executives involved.**

If you've had enough then actively start to look for companies that work with lower levels of complexity. They are out there! Maybe there is one where you can fully use your market expertise.

Provide feedback to your peers and bosses about what you think about those inhumanly high levels of complexity and, yes, vote with your feet!

Here's another key question: Can you identify fully with the products or services you or your company are selling? Do the products or services – which through your personal involvement in selling will always carry your personal energy – cause harm to other fellow beings?

Let us again take an extreme example. Say you work in an industry that produces arms or components for arms. Think through in detail what your company's products or services will be used for. I mean really picture it, even if you only work in manufacturing, finance or supply chain. In the end all arms are used for hurting and for killing people. Their use causes tremendous pain and sorrow. During the past 40 years over 60 per cent of all people killed in wars were civilians. And these are just the official numbers.

**Look carefully *where* your arms are deployed. One day they can be used to kill you and your own family. You never know. But you do know that their use is always destructive. Do you really want to be part of that?**

You see, it does matter how you earn your money.

I've heard it from senior executives who work in electronics manufacturing for arms that they are not responsible for the way politicians and the military use their weapons, and therefore, it does not matter how they are make their money. But the same executives would most likely protest immediately if someone, hypothetically, suggested that they recommend their daughter to become a prostitute or their sons to start a career in drugs dealing.

You see, in the case of their children it would matter how they made money. In business there's often this kind of dishonest ambivalence. If you are true and sincere, this ambivalence would not enter into the equation.

**If you sell products that have real potential to hurt or to do serious damage to others, that pollute the environment or, worst of all, can kill, cripple or debilitate other human beings, or which are specifically designed for any of the above purposes, you *are* partly responsible.**

Find a job in a different industry, where your sales talents have a value, and walk away. It's good for your soul.

One more thing: when you work in sales management, it is part of your strategic task to know your competitors well. Use this knowledge for yourself. If you want to change, don't just go for the firm with the highest reputation. Reputation can be lost in a single day.

Here's a small example: since the Fall of 2008, CV's of executives from some of the world's most prestigious investment banks were piling up on my desk. No-one wanted them, despite all their prestige. Many of them had made a grave mistake that only our ego would let us make: they had mistaken aggressive greed for reputation, which in the past had been socially accepted.

But let us not forget that we now live in tough and very decisive times.

It may therefore be smarter to go for a company where you like the attitude and style of their executives. Go for a positive, invigorating culture! Go for true human qualities and analyse what kind of personality succeeds in that firm. Ask yourself:

- Will they value your professional expertise as much as your personality?
- Is their management style constructive or abusive?
- How is target-setting organized; how strict or flexible are their bonus schemes?

We are all so used to "selling" ourselves (i.e. our energy, our health and in many cases our soul), but what for? Equally we are so used to fighting in order to maximize money and status, as if our whole life depended on it. How naïve and ultimately dangerous this could be.

Your life depends first and foremost on its quality. You, and nobody else, are in charge of maximizing that!

But if you want to fight, that's also fine. At least you should utilize your energy to fight for positive and constructive values, such as job satisfaction, meaningful content and a dignified workplace.

If you are in sales or sales management, I guess you got the gist of that. I have seen people change job or industry – indeed, I have helped many of them. Those who succeeded asked the right questions: not "How much can I earn?", but "Does this suit my talent and character?" With such questions in mind, success follows automatically. It always follows, and on more than just one level.

So, for the last time, dear reader, here are the three mission-critical questions we should all ask ourselves:

- **Does the work I do truly suit my talents and character?**
- **Does it match my personal vision of how I want to live?**
- **Does it make me happy?**

## Antidote No. 7: Reconstruct your image of the divine

It is now time to come full-circle. That is why we have to revisit the introductory part of this book in order to understand the full significance of what has been said so far and of what will be said now.

**The Devil's prime tool in creating and maintaining all negative energies and emotions in human beings is *fear*.**

The Devil as energy, by the way, is as real as are all your fears! The reason is that it is always your fears – and nothing else – that prompt you into acting either dishonestly, without dignity or without respect. In ancient terms: sinfully.

**Those fears were instilled, according to the Bible, into human beings at the time of the "fall from paradise". Before that event human beings completely trusted their God, trusted their life and had no fear at all. This is precisely why they lived in paradise!**

It pays to think deeply about that one.

Fear is used by politics to manipulate millions of people every day (just think of all the hype around terrorism). Even we in business and senior management use fear as a tool to keep people toeing the line. Fear is also still one of the prime mechanisms applied to domesticating (read "educating") our children, much as we do with animals.

When you are afraid you are so emotionally charged, that you can't think straight, can't take decisions, and can't listen to your intuition. The latter is the only source of information that wants nothing but goodness for you and is always available.

**Let us remember that originally the Devil, a forceful and frightfully creative energy, which planted that fear, a painful yet also primitive energy within *us*, and through *us*, just when we started to become human beings– and, probably just when God wasn't watching.**

Think consciously about who you serve whenever you fall into the trap of fear yourself or when you wield that weapon.

To be clear, I'm not against authority. I have to use it and do use it in my business, exactly as most readers will do in their businesses.

The difference is being aware of what we are doing.

Authority used with restraint and kindness does not hurt another person's soul. Seeing authority applied with wisdom and dignity, much as we envision a wise king such as King Solomon, can indeed lift the spirit.

If we allow it to happen, our fear can manipulate us into using authority to threaten, ridicule or intimidate in the most negative and destructive way possible. Sadly that is how authority is mostly used in business and politics these days.

**If the Devil created fear to keep us under his control why then should we reconstruct our image of the Divine? Why should we not fight fear first, aggressively wage war against the Devil? Because fear and war and the Devil are one! The Devil is not a physical person. The Devil is a being that lives off our energy and therefore *wants* us to have war and strife, needs us to be in fear, and the more the better!**

Let us take a step back and look at our history in order to understand this more clearly. Despite all claims to the opposite, the worst organisations when it come to exploiting fear as a weapon against humanity were, and still are, some of the organized, predominantly monotheistic, religions of our world. From the beginning they used fear in order to threaten human beings into an unjustifiably uncritical obedience of their dogmas. The fear they instrumentalized is the fear of authority.

Why did the organized religions do so much damage through this act? Because fear of authority is the ultimate fear – and God is the ultimate authority!

Instead of helping humans to find peace by trusting life, which after all is God's gift to us, they destroyed all the trust we – as a natural instinct – had in God and his wonderful gift.

If you portray God as an atrocious and vindictive energy that is so cruel as to condemn the most precious element of his own children, their soul, to an eternity in hellfire, it is no wonder that all of us have developed so many subsequent fears – including above all, the fear of dying.

Instil the fear of an atrocious God into children when their consciousness is just beginning to evolve, and you have crippled that psyche for the rest of its life. As every professional psychologist will tell you, fear stemming from that age or stage of development, remains imbedded in our psyche – until we die. Or until we consciously dissolve them!

But it's even worse.

Those fears later on directly influence the way we see life, our relationships and other people, and, of course, also the way we see business – and ourselves in business. That damage has been done to almost every one of us in Western society.

If you see God as an unforgiving entity, then society – and its key constituent part, business – will also be run by unforgiving rules and people, and business will indeed become war.

This situation will not change unless we wake up.

We wake up once we start to reconstruct our own image of the Divine. This constitutes an act of enormous liberation. It's no wonder that all organized religions in our Western societies try to prevent this from happening.

Fearing God – instead of trusting and loving Him as a wonderful friend – is the primordial fear from which all other fears follow.

Our views of business, of ourselves and of life as a whole will, however, change once we change our own view of the Divine – and it will change your life for the better.

Would you like some proof?

Everyone in business knows the difference between going into a meeting or a negotiation filled either with anxiety and apprehension or, alternatively, going into such a meeting filled with openness and self-confidence.

Which case will bring the better result? It's obvious.

**The difference is the level of fear. Openness and self-confidence will lift us up and will *always* make us more successful. Fear constricts us and limits our choices.**

The fear of failure is another primordial fear. All primordial fears, including the fear of death and the fear of pain, can be traced back to our initial fear of a cruel God.

**Psychologically the fear of failure in business is always associated with the fear of an all-powerful, negative over-father, a fierce authority figure, who has the power to hurt, destroy and punish us. The fear of having sinned or failed is so entrenched that we in turn not only punish everyone else, we punish *ourselves* all the time.**

You may not have looked at it this way, but it is nevertheless true. The strangest part, however, is that this fear is quite illogical.

The following hypothetical example may illustrate this.

Imagine you work in a tough corporate environment. Aggressive target setting is matched by a social fear of failure as an implicit standard in the corporate culture. Then when our boss sends us to a negotiation with a hard and ambitious target to achieve and we don't deliver, we feel absolutely devastated and threatened.

Why? Because we are deeply afraid.

**Superficially we may be afraid of being looked down upon, afraid that we have lost our chance for promotion, afraid of having disappointed our boss and so on. A tough and aggressive corporate environment is driven by and based on fear. You may hate it, but remember it was *you* in the end who accepted to live under such circumstances.**

You can still change it, however!

Back to our example: following your perceived failure in negotiation, at an even deeper level, you are afraid that you may get fired, triggering a subconscious fear of social punishment or even a subconscious fear of losing your livelihood.

Why?

Because at the deepest level behind – or rather below – this fear is the fear of starving; below that the fear of dying and below that level something even worse. Dying and then being sent to hell – that is the ultimate fear embedded in our psyche since childhood, at least in Western society.

All of this happens mostly subconsciously, but it happens nevertheless, and it happens continuously.

Back to our example with the negotiation: we all know that in the reality of business life not that much happens to us, either way – unless, of course, we completely screwed up on the negotiation. If, positively, you over-reached the target in that negotiation you will not suddenly get promoted because of your triumph.

Neither will you get fired nor your life somehow be threatened if, negatively, you did not reach that target. But subconsciously exactly these fears are triggered. And it will happen again and again, unless we recognize the mechanism at play.

Once you take a step back you will see that most of our fears are unrealistic (although they are deep-seated). They are illogical and most of them are imagined. Yet, in our psyche, the place where good and bad meet are very real.

Let us now look at the same situation from a different angle.

Imagine, by contrast, that you work in a social and business fabric where bosses are more mature and understanding. In your firm people truly try to help and support each other. In the negotiation process you trust that you had given your best, and at a very deep personal level you believe in positive energy and motivation as a standard of the corporate culture.

Your bosses see it the same way. As a result, in your psyche, you don't subconsciously expect punishment, even though you may not have reached your targets. Of course you are not happy, but you and your boss maintain a feeling of openness, avoiding unnecessary drama. You may both be quite disappointed, but in the end this was just a negotiation, not a duel for life.

It may be subtle, but the difference can be felt.

**Imagine for a moment a more mature business world run by senior executives chosen on a basis of true human qualities and wisdom, and their determination to change corporate standards accordingly. How much of our life energy would *not* be unnecessarily wasted? How much wasteful drama would *not* take place? How much pressure and unhappiness would *not* have to be experienced in our daily office life? How much smarter and more effectively could we live and operate in business?**

It is worth trying.

For example, during a tough negotiation meeting, you are confronted with a counterpart who starts getting aggressive and threatening, and who makes a big drama out of the negotiation, as if lives depended on it. If this happens, think about that person's likely belief system.

What is their view of the divine?

In that moment you will be able to look through them, maybe even feel compassion. You're sitting opposite a frightened child. Maintain your composure. Don't fall for their drama.

Once you can say "Dear God" and you actually believe in a dear, kind God, then you have made it. Your fear and stress levels will go down. A kind God will do everything to support you and the development of your soul, not punish you. It will help you, not destroy you. A kind God will even help your counterpart in the negotiation, trying to reach solutions which benefit both sides, because in the end a kind God loves everyone.

**Once that has become your firm view, the world around you will also change. Slowly at first, but you will be less nervous in business, less stressed, more effective, less defensive and more liked by your colleagues, your bosses and your clients. Because for you business is *not* war anymore. And furthermore because in daily reality no-one in business enjoys having to deal with aggressive people. They and their egos get on everybody's nerves.**

Many others may still be playing childish and immature business games. That's fine, let them. But for you it will be different. Increasingly people will want to deal with you, not the others. And that includes your boss, key clients and even the company board. For a simple reason: because it makes them feel better. This won't happen overnight, but it will happen rather quickly.

Can you imagine the positive effect this could have on you – and on everyone you deal with?

But remember, this will only be possible once you have reconstructed your own view of the Divine – and have addressed your fears.

The old, stern-looking guy who got you stuck in a cold world which makes no sense and who has turned away from you because you've sinned, a horrific authority figure we need to fear all our life – and beyond – has in my opinion nothing to do with the real Divine. Such a

God is nothing but a fabrication, dreamed up by people totally filled with fear themselves or by people with paranoia for control.

**But mind you, their dogma is nicely serving someone's purpose. Just remember *whose* purpose!**

**Bang! Now you've got it: the *Devil* needs us to have that view of the Divine!**

Without it all, those fear-based programs wouldn't work. And it is precisely those fear-based programmes that hamper the quality of our lives, which push us to forget our trust, that make us miserable.

**By contrast a dear God would *never* want his beloved children to see life and Him like this.**

**As was said before, remember that of itself the Devil has no power at all. Of all the beings on earth it is us humans, and *only* us, who provide the Devil with power.**

Without human fear on the planet and actions resulting from that fear, the Devil would not be here. Stones and trees are harmless. Animals, yes, they may sometimes appear to be cruel, but in reality they know no evil. Only we human beings do.

What does that say about our own chance for salvation, for redemption? It means absolutely wonderful news!

At any moment we have the power to say: Stop.

In this regard, more than just allegorically, we are the masters of our own, individual universe. Let us simply cease being a source of energy for the Devil. That's it, it's quite simple. Live a good and dignified life. Because you deserve it!

Don't care what others may think. They are in charge of their own lives to look after, while we are in charge of ours.

Unfortunately most people are primarily in charge of their unhappiness and frustration. We should respect them nevertheless. They are free to change any moment they decide to, just as are we.

And when you are in business, in meetings, in negotiations, don't be too tough; don't be too hard on yourself or on others. It isn't necessary.

In your job you can reflect an image of a Divine that is wise and kind, not of a Divine that is a sadist. How about a God loving you despite all your shortcomings, proud of you and filled to the brim with the immense joy to have you as His son or daughter?

> Too simplistic?
>
> Too philosophical?
>
> Too easy to do?

Maybe ? But then again, maybe not.

What have you got to lose?

PS: Dear reader! If the above strikes a chord of resonance, please DO let me know. I will always try to respond personally. You see, I was very open, honest and direct. This was not always easy and your feedback, even if it's only a few lines, will mean a lot to me. Approval, disapproval, encouragement to continue or criticism… all feedback is welcome.

Thank you!

**JRZyla**

Email me via:
jrz@themanagementlounge.com
or
jrz@ jrzyla.com

# Recommended viewings and readings

*What the...Bleep....Do We Know*
DVD by William Arntz, Captured Light Industries, 2004.

*Just For the Money*
By Adrian Furnham (Cyan/Marshall Cavendish, 2005)

*Weight Loss for the Mind*
By Stuart Wilde (Hay House, 2004)

*Principle-Based Leadership*
By Steven Covey (Simon & Schuster, 1999)

*Enough*
By John Naish (Hodder & Stoughton, 2008)

*Illusions*
By Richard Bach (Arrow Books, 2001)

*The Alchemist*
By Paulo Coelho (HarperCollins, 2006)

# About the author

Joachim Rene Zyla, 55, is ranked one of the most experienced European executives with a focus on Senior Management Evaluation.

After MBA and PhD studies in Vienna, Paris and at Harvard Business School in Boston, JR Zyla worked for almost 12 years in the investment banking industry, predominantly in London. In 1990 he moved into management consulting and in 1997 became CEO and key shareholder of Odgers Berndtson Central Europe (formally Ray & Berndtson CEE), the leading executive search company in the region.

In 2009 JR Zyla merged his company with Heidrick & Struggles, the world's largest leadership advisory business, where he still serves as a partner, on a part time basis.

Through his work with leading international companies JR Zyla has the advantage of having been able to study a large cross-section of corporate organizations of all sizes from the inside. These special insights allow him to take a witty, but equally critical look at the current state of affairs of our modern business life. JR Zyla delivers "Knowledge Sharing" seminars for Senior Executives across Europe.

Dr. Zyla invites readers to visit his website at: www.themanagementlounge.com or equally to contact him directly at jrz@jrzyla.com.